On Voting

THE LOCKE INSTITUTE

Founded in 1989, The Locke Institute is an independent, non-partisan, educational and research organization. The Institute is named for John Locke (1632–1704), philosopher and political theorist, who based his theory of society on natural law which required that the ultimate source of political sovereignty was with the individual. Individuals are possessed of inalienable rights variously defined by Locke as 'life, health, liberty and possession,' or, more directly, 'life, liberty and property.' It is the function of the state to uphold these rights since individuals would not enter into a political society unless they believed that it would protect their lives, liberties and properties.

The Locke Institute seeks to engender a greater understanding of the concept of natural right, its implications for constitutional democracy and for economic organization in modern society. The Institute encourages high-quality research utilizing in particular modern theories of property rights, public choice, law and economics, and the new institutional economics as a basis for a more profound understanding of important and controversial issues in political economy. To this end, it commissions books, monographs, and shorter studies involving substantive scholarship written for a wider audience, organizes major conferences on fundamental topics in political economy, and supports independent research. The Institute maintains a publishing relationship with Edward Elgar, the international publisher in the social sciences.

In order to maintain independence, the Locke Institute accepts no government funding. Funding for the Institute is solicited from private foundations, corporations, and individuals. In addition, the Institute raises funds from the sale of publications and from conference fees. The Institute is incorporated in the State of Virginia, USA, and has applied for non-profit, tax-exempt educational status under Section 501(c)3 of the United States Internal Revenue Code.

Officers of the Institute are listed above. Please direct all enquiries to the address given below.

4084 University Drive, Suite 103 • Fairfax, Virginia 22030, USA

On Voting

A Public Choice Approach

Gordon Tullock

Karl Eller Professor of Economics and Political
Science, University of Arizona

THE LOCKE INSTITUTE

Edward Elgar
Cheltenham, UK · Northampton, MA, USA

Published by
Edward Elgar Publishing Limited
8 Lansdown Place
Cheltenham
Glos GL50 2HU
UK

Edward Elgar Publishing, Inc.
6 Market Street
Northampton
Massachusetts 01060
USA

A catalogue record for this book
is available from the British Library

Library of Congress Cataloguing in Publication Data

Tullock, Gordon
　　On voting: a public choice approach / Gordon Tullock.
　　　(The John Locke series)
　　Includes bibliographical references.
　　1. Voting.　2.　Social choice.　I. Title.　II. Series: John Locke
series in classical liberal political economy.
　　JF1001.T84　1998
　　324.6'5—dc21　　　　　　　　　　　　　　　　　　97–30636
　　　　　　　　　　　　　　　　　　　　　　　　　　　　CIP

ISBN 1 85898 666 4

Printed and bound in Great Britain by
MPG Books Ltd, Bodmin, Cornwall

This book is respectfully dedicated to the Marquis de Condorcet, Charles Lutwidge Dodgson, and Duncan Black.

CONTENTS

CONTENTS

LIST OF FIGURES AND TABLES

Figures

Tables

ACKNOWLEDGEMENTS

The author wishes to acknowledge the administrative and secretarial assistance of Mr. Bryan J. Cash, Mr. Benjamin Shelledy, and Mrs. Viola Furry. In addition, Dr. Charles Rowley did his usual superb job of editing. He, in fact, made a number of helpful suggestions above and beyond the normal scope of editing.

CHAPTER 1
Introduction

We have all heard the tale of the drunk who was seen searching the ground under a street light. Upon being asked what he was doing he said that he was hunting for his lost key. On being further asked where he had lost it he pointed off in the dark stating 'over there.' They asked him why he was looking where he was, rather than where he had lost it, and he said 'There is more light here.' It is customary at this point for everybody to laugh at his stupidity, but it should be noted that if there is not any light where the key is, he probably could not find it there either.

Nobelist Peter Medawar was among other things a friend of Sir Karl Popper, and interested in the philosophy of science. He wrote a book called *The Art of the Soluble.*[1] Therein he argued very strongly that in science we do not try and solve the most important problems, we try to solve the problems which we think we can. In other words, the easier problems. In a way he is suggesting that we look under the street light, instead of off in the dark.

This may seem bad advice, but what if we are looking for not a single object like a key, but diamonds?[2] Suppose diamonds are thinly scattered over the ground. I think we could agree that looking where there is light would be the best way of finding diamonds. Science is some what like this, but we hope over time the area under the light will steadily expand.

What does all of this have to do with this book? In my opinion, 'public choice' has become too concerned with the areas where there is light, and too little concerned with expanding that area. Kuhn[3] wrote a very famous book in which he talked about revolutionary and normal science.[4] Revolutionary science is where you make a radical change and normal science is working slowly forward in a step by step way.

When public choice first started it was clearly a paradigm shift, or a revolutionary change in the way of dealing with political matters. It has over time become normal science. This is no insult as new information is developed and we become more certain of various things. In other words there is progress, but we don't now have revolutionary expansions.

I believe that the rent-seeking insight, which I am naturally very proud of, is bigger than the ordinary step forward, but not a true revolution. Perhaps we could call it a very small revolution. It has led to a large volume of material, but once again I think this is a normal science rather than a paradigm shift, once the first step was taken.

One objective of this book is to suggest that we go out of the area we have been working on, and try to create a new revolution, or at the very least increase the wattage of the light so we can see further out. There are a number of places where it seems to me we could validly expand our work. This book in a minor way does so expand it. More importantly, by somewhat changing the focus, and in particular, the scope of our studies, I hope to encourage research which will expand the area lighted by street lamps.

The Newtonian system, after all, was a great step forward even if we now think that in many areas it was less than perfectly true. Similarly, I have no doubt that the work being done now in public choice is development of a paradigm, and this development is worth doing. Still, I would like to move out of the existing area and into new areas which I have attempted in this book. However, I will concede that my progress is not gigantic. There are a few useful new models for areas that have previously not been dealt with in any way, but the revolution must await further work. I will be suggesting areas where I think we should do work rather than doing the work myself.

Of course there is a great deal of rehearsal of existing work. I have devoted my life to public choice, and tend to be emotionally attracted by it. In addition, it would not be possible to write the book without any reference to the existing work. The reader will find that I am not exactly exhaustive in my coverage of the existing work, and the book is rather lightly footnoted. This is because there is a considerable number of good general books in the field.

In science we always have the problem of whether we want a theory with considerable logical coherence and intellectual appeal or a catalog of facts. We should work on both and hope that as time goes by not only will we acquire more factual knowledge but that our theories will come closer to a complete explanation. Indeed, the theories very frequently will be the guides that lead to new information.

I will describe a number of political institutions which tend to be overlooked in most of the Public Choice literature. My former teacher and friend Sir Karl Popper argued that you start with theories, and then test them in the real world. He said he would not pay any attention at all where the theories came from. It seems to me that one of the sources of theories is knowledge of the real world.

The Greeks noticed that ships as they approached land became gradually visible. At first you could see tops of the masts and then what you could see would gradually work down until you could see the entire ship. They deduced from that the world was a sphere. When they made that deduction it was possible for them to make a number of observations to test it, and the tests turned out to be favorable. They even got a very good measure of the diameter of the sphere.

Here we have: first, observation of the real world; second, the creation of a theory to explain the observation; and third, empirical testing to find out whether the theory was correct in other areas. I think this is the history of most sciences.

In a recent issue of _The Journal of Economic Perspectives_, Michael Hanemann, said 'market prices are inappropriate measures of value. In the presence of externalities, market transactions do not fully capture preferences. Collective choice is the more relevant paradigm'.[5]

The first part of this, that market prices in the presence of externalities are not terribly good measures of value, is a statement that all economists will accept. His view that collective choices are necessarily better is rather old-fashioned and few people who have studied public choice would say that now. What we have are two different methods of making decisions, and both of them have serious defects. Fortunately the defects are to some extent asymmetrically arranged.

In other words, it may be possible to use the market where it is more efficient than collective decisions, and in another area where collective decisions are better, to use the government. We should keep firmly in mind that neither of these are perfect, and for that matter, neither is even close to perfection. For want of better alternatives we use them, but we should refrain from the kind of unthinking assumption that imperfection of one means that the other is better. It may be, or it may not. The world is an unsatisfactory place.

The reason for this repetition of elementary public choice here is that this book is mainly devoted to voting. The reader will find many difficulties with voting as he goes through it. I would not like him to come out of that with a view that the market is necessarily perfect. We will find difficulties with the voting process. There are equally severe difficulties with the market process, but that is not the subject of this book.

This book then, will concern voting, an important part of democratic decision making. To some extent, it is also used in dictatorial governments, because dictators frequently assign committees to make individual decisions, mainly in order to prevent individual contestants for the throne from becoming too strong. These groups normally make their decisions by voting although the dictator may overrule them.

Thus, voting procedures are important, and more important in democracies than in dictatorships, but not of total unimportance in dictatorships. They are also important in many other areas. Private clubs, corporations, and many religious organizations are examples. This book will attempt to cover the techniques of voting and their outcomes. We will also discuss how it is that some things are put up to a vote and others not.

From the viewpoint of professional public choice scholars, this book may seem in some ways rather elementary because I would like to have it readable to political scientists and others who are not fully familiar with the public choice literature. Thus, I frequently repeat things that the public choice scholar already knows, but I believe there is a great deal of original material as well. The author always has this problem whether he shall assume all of his readers know everything he does, or assume that they know nothing. The compromise I have selected may or may not please people in either the know all or know nothing camps, but it is the best I can do.

I will discuss a collection of voting procedures, including many that have not been given much formal analysis in the past. Further, I will attempt to cover a number of schemes that are actually used in the real world, but which are little known to American scholars. This is important because we get different results from the same set of individuals voting with the same preferences but with different voting methods.

There is one particular problem we will ignore. Small groups, let us say three members of the NKVD in an office in the Lubianka, glancing briefly at a file and deciding the future of a man they have never seen, are heavily dominated by the interpersonal relationships within the group. It is only when we go to very large groups that these interpersonal relationships tend to shrink in importance.

In this book I will be dealing mainly with groups which do not suffer any significant influence on the voting process by what we may call sociological relations among the voting population. This is merely a simplification to keep me out of the very difficult problems of small group dynamics. It may be hard for the reader to keep this in mind since I will frequently illustrate voting problems with examples in which there are only a few voters in order to make the discussion simple and the principle is intended to apply to large groups.

There will be cases where we are forced to turn to the problems posed by personal interconnections between the voters. In the real world they are sometimes very important, but mainly we will be dealing with situations in which large groups are voting, and interpersonal relations among the voters are of little importance.

When I say large groups I do not necessarily mean the entire population. The College of Cardinals, the Roman Senate, or for that matter the American Senate, are all examples of large enough groups of people so that we can assume the subject matter in this book will fit them.

We are going to be inclusive here. Not only are some of these voting bodies rather exclusive with only a few people out of the voting population permitted to vote, but if we look at the history there have been many cases where the individual voters have different weights; the modern corporation for example. We will also discuss this, but not in the early part of the book. There is also the relationship between those people who can vote and those who cannot. Historically, this has been of great importance, but largely unanalysed.

As a digression from the main work in the book, I point out that in those long lasting situations in which the franchise was restricted, but there was a vote (for examples, in Venice, Berne, and England during the Whig predominance). The people who could vote lived in unfortified and practically unguarded housing. In other words they were susceptible to mob violence. You rarely find this discussed in the literature, but surely they were aware of this, and would refrain from any line of policy which if continued for a considerable period of time might lead to being lynched.

Still, my intent is to examine the process of voting and not give it a moral evaluation. If the reader strongly believes in one person, one vote,[6] I shall not complain. From the standpoint of this book, however, the whole voting population of the US is simply one of a number of voting bodies, the US Senate is another. Both of them are large enough in numbers so that the interpersonal relationships tend to get drowned in the particular type of considerations that we will be dealing with.

There is another problem which is very important, and that is why individuals choose to vote for particular alternatives. In his famous book, *Social Choice and Individual Values*,[7] Arrow specifically says that his theory only applies where people are voting in accordance with their true preferences. This will be dealt with in more detail later, but for the first part of this book we will accept the limitations used by Arrow partly because more mathematical work has been done under those restrictions than the other rules, and partly because many people believe that is the way voting takes place. Most of us, of course, realize that people do not always vote their simple preferences. I would have prefered any one of several dozen people to either Clinton or Dole, but I did not vote for them.[8] It would be throwing the vote away.

More important, and another thing that Arrow specifically ruled out is that the individual may vote against his preference for A because he has been offered something in return for casting his vote for B.

I have a nice quotation from the man who is now Majority Leader of the House of Representatives. While still only a minority whip, he succeeded in getting out and to the floor for a recorded vote an amendment providing that farmers who had more than the 125,000 dollars income from non-farm sources should not receive crop subsidies. One would think that in a recorded vote no congressman would dare vote against it, but he lost 2 to 1. His comment was 'There are no weak sisters on the agricultural committee, they are very good at doing what committees do. They spend 5 years filling their silos with political chips, and when the time comes they call them in'.[9]

This is a field in which I think that I was the first person to engage in formal analysis, although the fact that it happened was well known, and informal discussion was found in some political science books. We will talk about it a good deal later on in the book.

In any event, we shall start by talking about those cases where the voters vote entirely in terms of their own preferences, then discuss the possibility of strategic voting, assuming that there are no trades or bargains made among voters. We will then discuss the situation which for most important political decisions is the dominant one, where the voters do engage in trades with each other. Very commonly they are voting in favor of A which they don't like, because they have been promised that if they do it they will get B.

There are other problems which will be taken up later. One of these complications which must be at least mentioned here, is the information held by voters. Economists, have for a long time argued that the models which assume that purchasers are perfectly informed are helpful, although I don't believe any teacher really believes that all of his students are perfectly informed.[10] Nevertheless, the perfect information assumption has turned out to be useful.

In general, those economists like Arrow, Duncan Black, Buchanan and myself, who began applying our tools to political science began with the same assumption. It was quickly realized that these assumptions were incorrect. Voters don't know very much, and, in fact, probably much less than purchasers in the market. This will be dealt with at greater length later.

That leaves one further basic problem. In a number of cases our voters will have preferences over a number of alternatives, that is the one they like best, and various others that they in varying degrees like less. In actual practice, with voting methods in which voters list their preferences, we frequently find they do not bother to list their lower level preferences. This probably indicates they don't have any real preference structure over the entire list.

Indeed, if the problem is one which is simply given to them quickly, they do know what they prefer now, but it may not be what they prefer 5 minutes from now. Public opinion polls frequently show sharp changes on a particular question if another questionnaire is administered a short time thereafter.[11]

All of these difficulties are to be taken up in this book. We will start with the simplest possible model; a model in which the voters vote according to their preferences without engaging either strategic voting or trades with other people. We will assume our voters are well enough informed, so that in any event their preferences are reasonably firm, and that they don't engage in bargaining.

As we go forward we will loosen these restrictions, bringing in more and more complications. With this move toward greater realism, we will discover there are more difficulties. It should be said that even with the simplest model there is a very serious difficulty which will be discussed in Chapter 3. This difficulty, the voting paradox, is well known to all public choice scholars. Nevertheless, I will explain it because I hope this book will be read by newcomers to the field as well as the specialists in the subject.[12]

To repeat, our analysis will apply wherever voting is used, whether the troika which determined the future of people who had the bad fortune to fall into the hands of the NKVD or a Swiss referendum. The reader should keep in mind, however, that very small groups may behave differently.

It should be re-emphasized that there are very many different ways of voting, and they may have different outcomes in any given situation. The choice among them is in many ways as difficult as the choice between the market and collective decision procedures. For example, President Clinton, is now President. If we had used the voting method used in The Netherlands and, until the last election, in Israel, he would not be, although it is possible he would have been able to negotiate a position as Prime Minister.

This is by no means the only example. Saari has proved that with any given set of preferences there is at least one voting method which will generate any outcome among those over which the preferences extend.[13]

This is a basic problem and indicates that when you refer to democracy, you are not being highly specific. I occasionally run into people who when presented with several different voting methods inquire which one is the most democratic. This depends upon the definition of democracy, and most people accept whatever method they have been brought up with as the most democratic. In other words, it is just a matter of tradition. Those who do not accept it tend to go for the Borda method,[14] which as far as I know is not used for political purposes. There are a number of clubs that use it, but no government.

Returning to the main topic of this book which is to discuss voting, we began by saying that there are many defects in the market which is the standard alternative. Charitable activities are a third possibility, and also have advantages and defects, but insofar as I know no one ever relies upon them to fully replace the market or government. Non-democratic government is also common, but will not be discussed here.[15]

We will discuss how voting, one broad category of decision-making processes, works without any assumption that it is ideal. On the other hand the alternative decision making processes of which we have knowledge are also far from ideal. Among the possible voting procedures, this book will not tell you which is best. Indeed, no one knows which is best. We will merely discuss the whole universe and let you make your own decisions.

---

[1] Medawar, Peter Brian. *The Art of the Soluble*. London: Methuen 1967.

[2] The Hope diamond was actually found by a man who stumbled over it by walking over a field.

[3] Kuhn, Thomas S. *The Structure of Scientific Revolutions*. Chicago: University of Chicago Press, 1962.

[4] He didn't use that terminology, but it is easier to understand.

[5] 'Valuing the Environment Through Contingent Valuation', *Journal of Economic Perspectives*, Volume 8, Number 4, Fall 1994, Pp. 19-43

[6] Normally, lunatics and criminals are left out.

[7] John Wiley, New York, Second and enlarged edition, 1963.

[8] Arizona has introduced a new way of voting, so I changed my habit, and voted.

[9] *Washington Post*, (August 9, 1990):A4.

[10] I have just finished grading a set of exams.

[11] This shift is not obvious in the published data, because they simply give you the aggregate. If A prefers X to Y on Monday, and Y to X on Tuesday, and B prefers Y to X on Monday, and X to Y on Tuesday, the result is you have one for each both Monday and Tuesday, and you don't realize that people have changed their position.

[12] My practice of explaining matters which public choice scholars find elementary may mean that specialists will want to skip those parts.

[13] 'Millions of Election Outcomes from a Single Profile', Donald G. Saari, *Social Choice and Welfare*, 9:277-306.

[14] Explained below.

[15] See my *Autocracy*, Martinus Nijhoff, Dordrecht, 1987.

CHAPTER 2
Myths

It may seem odd to have a chapter of myths at the beginning of what is intended as a fairly scientific approach to such an important problem as voting. The reason is that I have discovered almost every one in public discussion acts as if they believe very strongly in certain myths. Indeed, people will speak in mythological terms about matters when they themselves firmly know the facts. There appears to be something rather Platonic about it as if certain myths about our voting system are thought to be Platonic essences, and the realities are the Platonic accidents.

I would like to go through a little of my own teaching experience. I teach a course in Public Choice which there are some graduate and some undergraduate students, some economists and some political scientists. I regularly begin the course for students who have not yet done any reading by asking them whether they think majority voting is the best method of making government decisions. With almost no exceptions I get an agreement to this, although there are people who think the bill of rights should take priority over voting, or something of that sort.

Having acquired this general agreement, I say, 'of course, you people are all opposed to juries making their decisions by unanimous votes'. They are in immediate difficulties.[1] Sometimes they say that when long-term imprisonment is threatened, unanimity is clearly desirable. I usually point out that I found myself spending several years in more unpleasant conditions than at most prisons in the latter part of World War II as a result of an ordinary democratic vote without unanimity.

There is also the fact that to acquit requires a unanimous vote just as to convict. There is the fact that the same procedure is used in civil suits as in criminal suits[2] In recent years I have been pointing out that President Clinton did not have a majority of the populace behind him. I sometimes get an answer that he did have a majority of the electors. That is true, but the electors were elected by less than a majority. Further, Clinton is by no means unique in this respect. Both Lincoln and Wilson were elected by a minority of the voters. It is interesting that almost certainly Douglas in a two man fight could have beaten Lincoln, and either Taft or Roosevelt in a two man fight could have beaten Wilson. Once again my students look puzzled by all of this, but do not abandon their views that majority voting is the right thing to do and that juries should be unanimous. I suspect that to them our system is by definition majority voting, and it follows that whatever we do is majority voting.

I usually continue pointing out that in the senate of the United States, if the minority really objects, a 60 percent majority is needed. There is the fact that the two-house legislature with the two houses being elected in different ways means that a simple majority in each house, is equivalent to something like 55 to 60 percent of the vote in a one-house legislature. There is the further fact that the president can veto and is in essence a third house of the legislature. He can be overridden by two-thirds vote in both houses.

There are the provisions for constitutional amendment which are far from majoritarian, although in some state constitutions a simple majority in a referendum is all that is necessary. I am a resident of one such state (Arizona). If we go out of the United States, we find similar situations. The United Kingdom, for many years, has had three parties, with a result that whoever is Prime Minister normally represents between 40 and 45 percent of the voters, because the remaining vote is divided among the other two parties.[3] In this case, it is interesting the party that does worst, the Liberal Democratic Party, probably in a two party vote could beat either of the others. One would anticipate that in a vote between the Liberal Democrats and Labour most Conservative voters would vote Liberal Democrat, and in a contest between the Liberal Democrat Party and the Conservative, most Labour voters would vote for the Liberal Democrat. It also seems likely that the Liberal Democrat is the first choice for a great many voters who vote for one of the other two parties. They know that the Liberal Democrats are not going to win, and regard voting for them as throwing their vote away.

For many years after Indian independence, although not now, the Congress party regularly got something in the order of 40 to 45 percent of the popular vote, and this elected about 80 percent of the members of the legislature. In this case, the Congress party was a middle party, and the majority who voted for the other parties were divided between a series of small parties on Congress's right, and a series of small parties on Congress's left. It was only after Mrs. Gandhi imposed a short-lived dictatorship that it was possible to build a coalition of non-Congress parties, and push Congress out.

Russia, in her 1995 legislative election, showed a particularly bizarre effect. Russia had copied the German constitution in which one-half of the lower house legislature is elected by individual constituencies in the Anglo-Saxon manner, and the other half is elected by proportional representation. Enough votes are given in the legislature to each party so that their representation is equivalent to the percentage of their votes in the total population. There is also a rule that requires a party to achieve 5 percent of the vote in order to have any representation.

In Russia, it turned out that there were very many parties running, and the bulk of them did not make the 5 percent cut. The result was the parties that made the 5 percent rule, and got members of the national constituency represented only 51 percent of the voters. That's a majority, but a bare one. Further, the other half of the legislature was elected by individual constituencies, and a great many winners were independents without party affiliation.

It is not only the average person who has not thought about these matters who has difficulty. Dennis C. Mueller, who is past president of Public Choice Society, distinguished contributor to public choice literature and the author of a standard text which I use in my course.[4] also has problems. On pages 52–55 he discusses the 'optimal majority' and in it he explains the Buchanan-Tullock argument for somewhat more than a simple majority in most voting.[5] He even reproduces our figure. Immediately after that he turns to 'Section E', called 'simple majority as the optimal majority'. I am not going to repeat his argument in full, even though I am about to criticize it, but I will quote a couple sentences. 'Nothing we have said so far can indicate why $K/N = N/2$ should be the optimal majority for the bulk of a committee's decisions; and yet it is'. He then refers to another diagram in which he claims that less a majority vote is likely to be very expensive and difficult.

In order to explain this I should say a little bit about what the book _Calculus of Consent_ says about less than majority votes.[6] In general, for reasons to be explained later, we were in favor of more than a simple majority, but we argued that for unimportant matters it might be sensible to require less than a majority to save time. This is for unimportant matters. We never suggested that presidents be elected by 43 percent of the vote. Since less than majority was suggested only for unimportant matters we didn't elaborate.

I regret to say that this minor point has become almost a standard channel for attacking our line of reasoning. Critics point out that if one proposal gets less than a majority there may be another which gets more, and hence you would have an endless series of votes. They do not seem to notice that this was not what happened to Lincoln, Wilson, and Clinton.

I have great difficulty believing that anybody who was aware of things like American presidential or British parliamentary elections in which majorities are not necessary would think that endlessly repeated votes would necessarily happen with a less than a majority requirement. The matter will be discussed at more length in the later part of the book. Even if you did agree that less than majority requirements be ruled out by this absurd line of reasoning, that would have nothing to do with our argument that in important matters, more than a majority is desirable.

I was originally surprised at Mueller making this error, but this is the second edition of his book. It seems possible he discovered that he was getting enough criticism from conventional political scientists that it was necessary for him to ease off on the reasoning. It should be pointed out that, with the exception of the 'but it is', nothing he says is literally wrong, it is just that it gives the wrong implication. In more recent work[7] he seems to be returning to the reinforced majority.

It should be pointed out there are many cases where most people don't like simple majority voting. The basic purpose of the Bill of Rights is to protect various things from simple majority voting. If you take an extreme case, it seems likely in 1933 you could have gotten a majority of the German people to vote, not that the Jews should be killed, but that they should lose a good deal of their property, and perhaps be exiled.

At the time our constitution was drawn up you could have gotten a majority of the population[8] to ratify slavery. Opinion turned against it later. In both of these cases the majority could impose a very severe cost on a minority. We will see below a well functioning democracy limits that kind of cost.[9]

So much for this particular set of myths. The average person talking about our voting uses language that is very far from what actually happens, even if he has practical experience. This is not particularly surprising as in many areas we have been taught to say one thing and do another. We will see later the statement that democracy reveals the 'will of the people' assumes that first, there is such a will, and secondly, the voting system works vastly more efficiently than it does. That is another myth but it cannot be dealt with here.

My final discussion here has not to do with myths about our present situation, but about myths about the past, and for other countries. Many students appear to believe that the word 'democracy' means a government in which all adults, with the possible exception of criminals and lunatics, are permitted to participate in the voting process. This is more or less true of most modern democracies, but if we want to make any use at all of historical data, we have to realize that it was not true before (at the earliest) the beginning of this century.

Here we are going to talk about voting methods including those cases in which not everyone can vote; indeed we will include even some cases in which only a relatively few people can vote, the Supreme Court for example. That is the reason this book is called *On Voting* and not *On Democracy*.

Speaking personally, I normally use the word democracy much more broadly than the average person does. I am willing to concede that substantially any place where decisions are made by voting, and the number of the people voting is above a low minimum and the voters are not subject to compulsion, is a democracy. But this is not the general usage of the term, hence I am referring to this book as a book on voting and not a book on democracy. Those of you who prefer to discuss only cases in which everyone, more or less, can vote, can follow the reasoning, but apply it less broadly.

It is interesting that although we make this sharp distinction we do not normally discuss it. I know of no place in which the question of why, let us say, the citizen of India should not be permitted to use his vote to influence the American aid program for India is even discussed. I presume most of my readers regard this as a question which should not even be asked, hopelessly foolish, or something of that sort. England gave most of the subjects of the king emperor their independence in the years right after World War II. They could have simply permitted them to vote for members of the House of Commons instead. They chose not to.

In my opinion, the reason is fairly simple, they were selfish. They did not want to be taxed to transfer large sums of money to India. Since I feel this way about permitting Indians to vote in American elections, this is not stated as a criticism. If there is any other argument for this geographic restriction of voting, I would appreciate hearing it.

A minor incident in my life will illustrate the point. I was giving a lecture at a university and one of the members of the regular faculty, anxious to bait a visiting conservative, came over to me and said: 'Do you think that illegal aliens should be permitted to vote?' I responded, 'I don't see why their location on one side or the other of an arbitrary line on the map, the Mexican boundary, should make any difference.' He paused, looked confused and said: 'I suppose that we should let all Mexicans vote.' Paused again and then said: 'I'd better think the whole subject over' and departed. I am sure that he purged the entire conversation from his memory very quickly.

I am not, of course, suggesting that we do let people who are much poorer than we are vote and hence tax us to transfer money to them. I am simply pointing out that the subject is normally not discussed, and that the only reasons that I know of for preventing this from happening is the purely selfish one that we do not want to be over-taxed by the world's masses.

Returning to the general question of who can vote within a national boundary, it is only in this century (except for a few western states that got in a little early) that women were permitted to vote. The 'some adult males can vote' has been the standard 'democratic' rule throughout most of history. Usually criminals and lunatics are kept out of the electorate.

To take an obvious case, in Athens foreigners and slaves could not vote. Foreigners in this case were defined as people who were not Athenian citizens and they could be the descendants of great-grandparents who had moved to Athens. Present day Switzerland puts very extreme restrictions on foreigners becoming citizens even though almost a quarter of the labor force are foreigners in Switzerland on labor permits.

The United States from the time of the first colonies was really quite open about permitting adult white males to vote. The situation differed from state to state and there were always at least some people who could not vote, but most adult males were permitted to vote in most colonies. The same situation continued after the Declaration of Independence and up to very recently.

But note that this was basically white males not black males. While the blacks were slaves, oddly enough, sometimes they were permitted to vote (i.e. their owner would march them all down to the polling booth and say: 'Here are fifty votes for so-and-so'). I doubt that the slaves drew much consolation out of this operation and it was unusual.

It is interesting that in the period right after the Civil War substantially all black males could vote, but a great many whites who had been too closely associated with the Confederacy could not. As the restrictions were relaxed the movement towards the old solid south occurred. The Jim Crow legislation, including the restrictions which effectively prevented blacks from voting in the south, was put through at a time when, at least at the beginning, the blacks could vote. They were, of course, outnumbered by the whites after the immediate post civil war years and only regained full voting rights in the 1960's. Thus, there has been no time in the United States up to 1960 in which there was truthfully universal adult suffrage with the usual exception of lunatics and criminals.[10]

It is interesting that during the period when the Jim Crow legislation was being put through, and blacks in the south were being deprived of their vote, white women were acquiring the vote. Hence, the total number of people who could vote probably increased throughout this period as the blacks were removed from the voting roll in the south and women were added.

People who want to talk only about democracy and insist that it is not democracy unless substantially all adults can vote must argue not only that Athens was not a democracy, but that Washington, Jefferson, Madison, Lincoln, and for that matter, Wilson and Franklin Roosevelt, were all presidents of a country that was not a democracy. I doubt that any of them will. The standpoint of this book is that the actual mechanics of the voting process, unlike the outcome, are not greatly affected by the number of the people who can vote.

There is one effect which reducing the size of the voting population does make on the outcome. The larger the number of people voting the less the influence of any single vote. It seems probable that people will give somewhat more attention to their vote when the number of other voters is low than when the number of other voters is large. On the other hand, in the modern circumstances of television, newspapers, etc. the intense coverage of things like the presidential election may mean that the voters give more attention than they would in a much smaller constituency.

A number of rather well functioning governments in the past have had quite restrictive voting rules. To name three, Venice, which had history's longest lasting successful government without coup, and Berne, which is in the second place, are examples of aristocracies with usually under one-quarter of the adult male population doing all the voting. It is arguable that England during the Whig predominance was another example.

I do not think that we can draw a great deal of guidance from this because it may be that these are simply a small sub-sample of a much larger collection of countries that had this kind of voting and most of which failed. Historical investigation here would be desirable, but it requires more linguistic ability than I have.

Let us turn to a few other matters connected with who should vote. The first of these is a suggestion that from time to time comes up in the public choice literature which is that instead of having our present kind of legislature, we simply draw a large number of people at random. They could be put in office for one or maybe two years and make all the decisions that are now made by our legislatures. The number would have to be fairly large to get a good random sample. The number in the jury is obviously too small.[11] Athens and the other Greek 'democratic' city states made much use of this method.

I find that my students all regard this as a totally lunatic idea, but have very little in the way of concrete objections to it. 'It's impractical,' is the most common single comment that I get. I suspect that is what most of the readers of this book will feel so also. We have not yet begun discussing what actually happens in legislatures, so I can at this point only say that this would be very different from normal legislatures. Whether this is an advantage or a disadvantage I will leave to the reader after he/she has finished the book.

Another method of getting somewhat the same result is permitting people to vote directly by referendum on various policy matters. I have noticed that people are beginning to say that Switzerland is not a representative democracy because they use direct voting so much. The same might conceivably be said of California. Note that there has to be some kind of decision as to exactly what they will vote on. This will be discussed again later.

There is also the question of how old you have to be to vote. F.A. Hayek at one point was talking about having one house of the legislature composed only of people who had been elected by a very senior electorate. At the other extreme right after World War II, a tribal government in New Guinea set up a small organization intended to be American style, in which everybody over the age of ten could vote. As a larger more practical example, before World War II, the electorate in Japan was all males over the age of 25.

For quite some time, the United States allowed men over 21 and women over 18 voting rights. The combination of a Supreme Court decision and a constitutional amendment switched this to 18 for everyone. I should point out that when we are talking about the age at which you begin to be able to vote, it is not all that clear that lowering the age limit benefits the younger people. If we lower the minimum age of voting from 21 to 18 this would mean that the people over their lifetime can begin voting at 18 rather than at 21. But in turn there are more people voting and hence, the influence of a single vote goes down. The question will be discussed at some length later. Another proposal that is sometimes made is that older people be deprived of the vote. This would have absolutely immense effects on our 'entitlements.' So far as I know, no one is seriously suggesting it.

Another suggestion that I sometimes run into is that there be minimum intellectual qualifications for voting. The strangest case that I ever ran into was a young man from MIT, who thought not literally that only people from MIT could vote, but something not too far from that.

I asked him why and he said that they would cast better votes and as an example suggested that bright students would get better fellowships and scientists more research money. It was not clear that he realized that he was advocating his own interests. It would appear that the principal objection to limited franchises is the fear that the voters would exploit the non-voters.

There is of course the prospect of giving people an exam before they are permitted to vote. No one, as far as I know, is particularly in favor of it, although Mueller has seriously suggested it[12]. It might be a good idea if you design the exam properly, but one can readily imagine cheating by the people who designed the exam. I was a China specialist at one time and China for some 1000 years selected all of their higher civil servants by a very, very difficult exam, which apparently worked quite well.

There is another question, which is seldom dealt with, which is how many votes individuals should have. Nevil Shute and the wealthy Mr. Hunt both wrote novels in which the world was saved by the fact that different people had different numbers of votes with, needless to say, the better people having more than one. As far as I can see the idea has never been advanced except in fiction.[13]

It is not true that the weighting of votes in existing democracies is always the same. As a very obvious case the influence of a citizen from Alaska on the Senate of the United States is radically greater than the influence of a citizen of California.

The Supreme Court decided that a similar difference between the upper and lower house of the legislature violated the United States Constitution for states, but did not believe that the same institution for the federal government violated the federal constitution. Since the particular clause that the Supreme Court depended upon had been written almost a hundred years before they reached this decision, and had never previously been interpreted in this way, this was simply one more example of the Supreme Court deciding that its view of the constitution should be guided not by the constitution but by advanced progressive thought.

The United Kingdom actually has an upper house which is partly hereditary and partly appointed. Somewhat similar arrangements were made in Canada and Australia, although their upper houses are not hereditary. It should also be pointed out that in England the Scottish constituencies are so arranged that the Scottish vote is somewhat more heavily weighted than an English vote. The only real explanation I can think of for this is that Scotland tends to vote Labour.

One area in which weighted voting is standard is the corporation, in which the number of shares you hold determines your vote. A number of condominiums have something like this. The large apartment building in which I lived in Washington D.C. had apartments of different size and expense. The number of votes that you could cast depended on what kind of apartment you were occupying. The condominium development in which I now live in Tucson has similar houses and there is no weighting of this sort, but we vote by houses. This means that I, an unmarried person, have as many votes as either of my next-door neighbors who are husband and wife teams. Another family a couple of doors down has an adult son, and they also have only one vote among the three of them.

The question of what one should vote on, that is, whether one should have a lot of local governments or a central government is also up for grabs.[14] Which officials should be elected rather than appointed. The Confederate Army in the Civil War had the soldiers elect officers up to the rank of captain. Since there is no doubt that the Confederate Army on a man for man basis outfought the Northern army, this may be evidence that this is a good idea.

Most standard military theory argues that you cannot have elected officers. But the Roman army, which by tradition was the best of all armies, was commanded under the Republic by consuls, who were elected officials. The equivalent of a regimental commander or colonel was normally a young man of good family who had been elected by the Roman assembly. To repeat, this was by tradition history's best army, and certainly these elected officers did very well in commanding their troops. To repeat, you can have elected officers.

There are others rules that are used at one place or another, or some time or another. A.V. Dicey, for example, was very disturbed with the British government when it set up a pension scheme for certain older people who retained their vote. He pointed out that up to that time people who were receiving pensions or other aid from the government could not vote. Today, going back to the old system would be a most remarkable change, with a considerable part of the American population, nearly 20 percent being deprived of their vote. Whether it would lead to a better government is another matter.

I have suggested in class that civil servants and their families be deprived of the vote. My argument was that either they voted like every one else, in which event the number is large enough so that removing a random sample should not change the outcome, or they tended to vote to improve the power, prestige and wages of civil servants. If it was the latter obviously democracy would work better if they didn't vote. Further, they would all be people who have voluntarily given up the vote.

It used to be true, and to a considerable extent still is true, that military people don't vote in the United States. There is no law that says they can't, but the administrative structure tends to prevent them from voting. This is particularly bizarre as the army surely could get larger appropriations in various ways if they arranged to have their people vote.

Now that the army is not drafted it is likely that the congressmen who wanted to pick up the votes of the neighboring military installation would in their speeches express desire to expand the military budget. Unfortunately or fortunately the military high command structure apparently hasn't figured this out. Back in the days when the army was largely drafted it might have been rather dangerous for them to permit the rank and file voting.[15] They couldn't prevent it, but they could refrain from encouraging it.

I will not discuss here the question of whether people value their vote, or whether they should value their vote, or whether they should cast well-informed votes. I am mainly talking here about what I refer to as the myths, and among the myths is one that our method of voting is the only way. This is emphatically not true. We will later discuss a number of other methods which have been used in voting in various parts in the world.

The basic theme of this chapter has been that a great many things are thought to be true by the average person about voting which are not. These are the myths that I have described. We will now turn to the actual situation rather than what you learned in high school civics.

---

[1] The reader may also find himself in difficulty.

[2] Some of the states use less than a unanimous vote in civil suits.

[3] On May 3rd 1996 in a vote for local officials all across Britain the Labour Party got 44 percent of the vote. The *New York Times* story on it (May 4, p.3) was illustrated by a picture of the Labour Party leader beaming at his 'triumph'. The *Times* correspondent apparently agreed that this meant that Labour would completely dominate the next parliament.

[4] Mueller, Dennis C. *Public Choice II*, a revised edition of Public Choice, (Cambridge, England: Cambridge University Press) 1989.

[5] Buchanan, James and Gordon Tullock. *The Calculus of Consent: Logical Foundations of a Constitutional Democracy*. Ann Arbor: University of Michigan Press, 1962. Translated into Spanish and Japanese in 1980 with Russian and Chinese translations forthcoming.

[6] 52–57.

[7] Mueller, Dennis C. *Constitutional Democracy*. New York/Oxford: Oxford University Press, 1996.

[8] The Blacks were not permitted to vote, but if they had been, there were not enough of them to change the outcome.

[9] It is amusing that the author of 'We hold these truths to be self evident, that all men are endowed by the creator with certain inalienable rights' was himself a large scale slave-holder. It even seems likely that he had one of his household slaves in the room at the time he wrote it.

[10] The Supreme Court has on occasion shown signs of feeling that lunatics and criminals should be able to vote too.

[11] It is notable that the Athenian jury for criminal cases was 401 which is roughly the same as our House of Representatives.

[12] *Constitutional Democracy* Op. cit.

[13] In England before World War II, some university graduates had two votes. Shareholders in companies normally have plural votes.

[14] My *New Federalist* London: Frazer Institute, 1994 is devoted to this issue. Originally published in 1992 in Serbo–Croation. Also translated into Russian and Korean in 1994 with a Italian translation forthcoming.

[15] The army of the Roman Republic was drafted.

CHAPTER 3
Some Simple but Confusing Mathematics

Most people thinking about voting assume there are no mathematical problems of any sort. You simply add up the votes, and that is that. Under modern circumstances the voters may directly communicate their wishes to a machine which then produces the outcome automatically. Unfortunately, it is not that simple. Various puzzles in connection with the mathematics of voting have disturbed a great many people, and caused a great deal of difficulty. A great many people, including at least two Nobel Prize winners, have done research in the area without really clearing it up.

The readers of this book should now be divided into classes. There are those who know a great deal about Public Choice, and who are fully familiar with most, although not quite all of this chapter. In general they should skip immediately to Chapter 4, although perhaps an approach which is different from the normal one might interest them. Readers who don't know about these problems should read this chapter as background for the rest of the book. The reader would make up his mind into which category he falls. The book is intended to be readable by people who are not students of the area, and hence does contain some things which will bore the specialist.

I am not going to repeat Arrow's theorem. I am going to produce a proof of my own which reaches much the same result, but not in as general a form as Arrow's theorem. We will use some of his conditions, but not all, and introduce another condition of my own. The end product is a much simpler proof, albeit not as general.

Arrow's conditions are first, that the voting method be decisive, that is it either tells you which alternative is preferred or possibly that they are tied. Second, that the voters may have any preferences, in other words we do not have a voting system that will work well only if the voters have a certain set of preferences. Third, not mentioned but implied by Arrow, is that they actually do have preferences over all of the alternatives, although informed indifference would be counted as a preference. They are not ignorant or uncertain.

The fourth condition is that there are at least 3 alternatives. The fifth, and this is not in Arrow and is the reason that my proof is simpler, is that whatever the voting method that is proposed, if it is used to select between only two alternatives it will select the one that is preferred by a majority of the voters. This particular proof will not cover all the voting methods discussed in this book, but it will cover all those in common use.

The final condition is simply that the voting method should not generate paradoxes, of which there are two usually discussed. One is intransitivity, A is preferred to B and B is preferred to C, but then C is preferred to A, and the second is a rather complicated condition which Arrow gave the uneuphonius title of 'lack of independence of irrelevant alternatives.'

This condition is usually illustrated by a little story about a man who goes into a restaurant and asks what they have for dinner. The waitress says: 'We have roast beef and chicken'. The man says that he will have the roast beef. She then says, 'Oh, I forgot we also have lobster.' He responds, 'Well, that is entirely different, if you have lobster, I'll have the chicken.' Immediately we would come to the conclusion that the man has something wrong with him and that he should consult a good psychiatrist. It is unfortunate that all known voting systems have this kind of defect, that is the choice between *A* or *B* may be effected by whether *C* is present even if *C* itself has no chance of being selected as the first preference.

I should say that this particular explanation of the 'lack of dependence on irrelevant alternatives' tends to annoy mathematicians who use a more general definition. The cases in which the more general definition applies (and this one that I have just given does not) are all cases in which the actual outcome of the election is not effected. Thus I prefer my definition of this particular category, but if the reader wishes he can use the broader definition, if he knows it. It will make no difference here.

In order to demonstrate what goes on I would like to begin by a very simple explanations of both of these problems. The first of these problems is shown in Figure 3.1.

Voters

	1	2	3
Preference	A	B	C
Rankings	B	C	A
	C	A	B

Figure 3.1: Intransitivity

If we follow the standard rules of order and we wish to select one of these we take two of them, let us say *A* and *B*, and hold a vote, in which as you can see by looking at the table, *A* beats *B*. We then put the winner of that against the third alternative, *C*, and once again as you can see by looking at the table *C* wins. The problem is that *B* can beat *C*. This is called a cyclical majority.

We are going to go into the frequency with which this might occur later but I can say here that if there are three alternatives and three voters who have preferences which are completely independent of each other, they would turn up about eight percent of the time. As the number of alternatives rises the likelihood of such a cycle increases quite rapidly and it also increases, only more slowly, as the number of voters is increased.

There is a sort of variant on this, which I call tie intransitivity, which is shown on Figure 3.2. In this case if you work out the votes you will discover that A is tied with B and with C, but that B beats C. This is a less extreme variant of the same problem.

Voters

	1	2
Preference	A	B
Rankings	B	C
	C	A

Figure 3.2: Tie intransitivity

We will now turn to an illustration of the lack of independence of irrelevant alternatives; a phenomenon that was actually first discovered in connection with scoring track meets, but is important for voting too. Borda, who I mentioned before, invented a method of voting, which is illustrated in Figure 3.3.

We have five people here and once again three alternatives and their preferences are as shown. Borda suggested that we give in this case different numbers according to their rank in the preferences. For example for Mr. 1, C could get zero points, B one, and A two. Borda then suggested that these all be added up and the one with the largest number of points would be the winner. It was almost immediately pointed out that there were reasons why it might be strategically wise to falsify your listing of preferences.

Borda responded to this by saying that the method was designed for honest men. We will turn to strategic maneuvering in a later chapter, so that can be left aside, but there is another serious problem here.

Voters

	1	2	3	4	5
Preference	A	A	A	B	B
Rankings	B	B	B	C	C
	C	C	C	A	A

Figure 3.3: Borda's method of voting

If the reader goes through Figure 3.3, he will realize that in a Borda vote A would get six points, B would get seven, and C would get two. Thus B wins. Suppose, however, that C decides that since she cannot win anyway, she will not even participate. In these circumstances with C not there, B would get two votes and A would get three, hence A wins. In other words, the choice depends on the presence or absence of a third candidate who, in this case, has no chance of winning. The lobster does make a difference.

There now remains the proof that no voting method will pass all of our conditions. In order to pass the conditions you must do so with any preference ordering. In 1949 in Russia substantially anyone given the choice between voting for Stalin and being left alone, or voting for anyone else and dying unpleasantly, would have preferred the first and hence any voting method would have worked in these circumstances. We want a system that works with any ordering of preferences and hence all that is necessary to disprove any given voting method's ability to do so is to simply show that with some particular ordering of preferences the paradox occurs.

Let us suppose that someone alleges that they have a voting method which meets our conditions regardless of the ordering of preferences. It should work with preference ordering in Figure 3.1. It is easy to show that it does not. Suppose that the person who has this method says that it selects one alternative as a winner, let us say A. It is easy to demonstrate that if B (the lobster) is removed then C will win, so this fails the test in this case.

But ties are always possible suppose that this voting method provides a tie, let us say between A and B. If we remove C which gets us down to two choices, this immediately makes A the winner, so here again the lack of the lobster is important. Finally suppose that the method in this particular case we are told provides a tie among all three. In this case the removal of any one means that there is a clear-cut winner between the other two.

Thus, all of these cases produce a different winner if you remove an alternative which is not itself the winner. In other words once again, the lobster makes a difference.

Let me now turn to giving you a few examples of real-life voting methods and demonstrate how they fail with respect to this proof. The first and simplest method, which is in many ways the oldest, is the way that individuals are elected to the House of Commons. This was mentioned in the last chapter, but it can stand further discussion. Any number of candidates who choose to put up a small deposit are put on the ballot. Since there, more often than not, are three candidates for any seat, Labour, Liberal Democrat, and Conservative, the winner may not and in fact characteristically does not have a majority of the votes. It is normally, although there are occasional exceptions, either Labour or Conservative.

If we arrange the things so that the voters vote on the candidates in pairs, it is fairly certain that the Liberal Democrat Party with its centrist position could beat the Conservative Party because they would have the Labour Party votes, and could beat the Labour Party because in a two-sided fight they would have the Conservative votes. Thus, this voting method does not produce the same result as would be obtained if we took only two. It should be pointed out that more often than not the House of Commons does have a majority in it.[1] This majority characteristically does not represent a majority of the voters.

Our system which involves electing electors who then vote for the Presidential candidate has in all cases except the third election turned up a majority in the college of electors but not popular majorities. Lincoln, Wilson, and Kennedy[2] all had less than a majority.

In Lincoln's case, it is fairly certain that if Douglas had met him on a two man fight, he would have won easily. As a matter of fact there were two other candidates and they weakened Douglas to the point that Lincoln won, even though he had no majority of the votes. In the case of Wilson, the situation is even stronger, as it seems likely that either of his two opponents, Taft or Roosevelt, could have defeated him, had they fought him on a man to man basis.

There is a variant of this simple plurality system which was used for quite a while in various states in the South and has been used elsewhere. In this system if no single candidate gets a majority the two top ones are put against each other and one of them necessarily will get a majority there. It can easily be so that the third choice could easily beat the one who wins in a vote restricted to the top two. The choice among Liberal Democrat, Labour, and Conservative in England mentioned above would be an example.

Louisiana had an interesting governor's race a few years ago in which Governor Edwards, well known to be a crook, turned out to be one of the two leading people in the primary with the other being Duke. Another man that probably could have beaten either easily in a two man contest was the third. This led to a contest between Edwards and Duke with bumper stickers that said 'vote for the crook not the Cook'. Edwards won. This would be a case in which the electorate chooses roast beef when the lobster is present and chicken when it is not, but if given a choice in pairs it would choose the lobster over the chicken or the roast beef.

There are many people who, observing ordinary voting particularly in the United States but in other countries that have the single member system too, are under the impression that regularly the choice is between two candidates or two measures. In legislative proceedings the rules of order require that matters be voted on in pairs. For example suppose the status quo is A in figure one proposal to change to B is made and then somebody offers an amendment which is C. These are now voted on according to the rules of order, which means that they are forced into pairs and C is defeated by B and B is defeated by A. This matter will be discussed at some length later.

The problem here is that the order in which they are voted on may be determinate. The method of switching to two for each stage determines the outcome. If the preferences were as in Figure 3.1 then if A had been voted against B and then the winner against C, then C would have won. Directly voting on the order in which they will be put simply reproduces the same cycle.

I should deviate briefly to talk about Condorcet. We have been specifying sets of preferences to make up our examples, but of course they are not the only ones that can occur in the real world. It may happen that there is one alternative which can get a majority in two-way votes against each of the others. This is called the Condorcet choice. When there are number of alternatives, and voters preferences are both determined and independent of each other, this would be quite rare.

It is not obvious that in the real world the voters preferences are independent or determined and other procedures that occur before the formal vote may whittle down the number of alternatives. These other procedures, which will be discussed at length later, are not in any sense more respectable than direct voting and may lead to results that are markedly inferior to what the people would choose if given different choices.

As the final example here let us turn to the standard American Presidential contest. Let us assume that it is one in which there is no third party or possibly that the third party is one of these tiny parties like Prohibition or Socialist, and that the number of votes they get do not deprive the winner of a majority.

The problem here is that we must take the whole procedure into account. The average voter voting in a primary takes into account both the degree to which the candidates in his party are in agreement to him and their likelihood of winning. Thus he is apt to vote for somebody that is closer to the other party than his own personal preferences. I will discuss this situation with much detail later under the rubric of single peak preferences. Turning to the actual election, consider the 1960 Presidential race. In the build-up to the nomination there were four candidates; Nixon and Rockefeller for the Republicans and Kennedy and Johnson as Democrats. In the general view of almost everyone Nixon was to the right of Rockefeller and Kennedy to the left of Johnson. Granted the eventual very close outcome of the election it seems absolutely certain that Johnson could have won with ease against Nixon and Rockefeller could have won with ease against Kennedy. Both, however, were eliminated and the fight was between Nixon and Kennedy.

I do not know what would have happened had Rockefeller been put against Johnson, but it is clear that the two strongest candidates, the ones most likely to get an easy majority, were eliminated in the first round. This is hardly what would have occurred had we gone through the complete set, that is Kennedy against Johnson, Nixon and Rockefeller then Nixon against Johnson and Rockefeller then Johnson against Rockefeller. If there was a Condorcet choice, this would have produced it and it would have been either Rockefeller or Johnson.

The problem was first discovered by two members of the French Academy, M.J. Condorcet, and J.C. Borda just before the French Revolution.[3] Condorcet died as the result of some difficulties with

Robespierre over voting methods. The problem will be described shortly, but we should say that it led to a considerable literature by other distinguished savants in the period from the end of the eighteenth into the early nineteenth century.

This general line of research sort of died out. People lost interest and forgot it. The same thing happened when the problem was rediscovered later. I should perhaps speculate a little bit about the reasons. The first obvious reason is that this whole problem raised deep questions about the validity of the democratic process. People who were devoted to democracy naturally did not want to consider it. The second problem is that it is very hard to find any examples in the real world where the problems seem to have had an effect. It is not that we can prove that they do not, but it is very difficult to prove that they do, even if only occasionally.

The problem in any event was forgotten and was rediscovered by Lewis Carroll (Charles Lutwidge Dodgson), of all people. Like so much of his important work it never actually reached the attention of the public. It is a tragedy that a man who could have revolutionized logical theory is thought of as the writer of two, admittedly brilliant, childrens' books.

The problem was then basically rediscovered by Duncan Black, who at that time was simply an obscure professor of economics and when he had his results published[4] they had relatively little impact on the world. His reputation has suffered somewhat because as an honest and industrious man he proceeded to rediscover Condorcet, Borda, and Carroll's work in the field.

The paradoxes obtained a good deal of notoriety and importance when Kenneth Arrow, a Nobel Prize winner, who wrote a book[5] containing a proof that no voting method that meets a rather limited set of obvious conditions can be constructed. In other words, voting is inherently paradoxical. This caused a fairly big outburst of interest and a great many articles were written. I would say that the bulk of articles, although they took the form of elaborating the theorem, were in fact trying to demonstrate that democracy did not suffer from the apparently hopeless defects that Arrow's theorem implied. All of this was in the early 1950s, through the 1960s, and into the early 1970s. Once again the subject has died out; in my opinion, for the two reasons that I gave before: that it challenges democracy and all the people that wrote on it were fervent democrats, and the fact that it is very difficult to find real life examples of its occurrence. But once again that is my opinion and I cannot prove it.

In order to not leave the reader in suspense, I should say that in my opinion the proof that democracy under Arrow's conditions is impossible is correct, but these conditions contain several which are not realistic if we look at the real world.

It has been stated above that the present study confines itself to the formal aspects of collective social choice. The aspects not discussed may be conventionally described as the game aspects, especially since that term has acquired a double meaning. In the first place, no consideration is given to the enjoyment of the decision process as a form of play. There is no need to stress the obvious importance of the desire to play and win the game as such in both economic behavior and political. That such considerations are real and should be considered in determining the mechanics of social choice is not to be doubted; but this is beyond the scope of the present study.

The other meaning of the term 'game' is that which has been brought to the attention of economists by Professors von Neumann and Morgenstern. The point here, broadly speaking, is that, once a machinery for making social choices form individual tastes is established, individuals will find it profitable, from a rational point of view, to misrepresent their tastes by their actions, either because such misrepresentation is somehow directly profitable or, more usually, because some other individual will be made so much better off by the first individual's misrepresentation that he could compensate the first individual in such a way that both are better off than if everyone really acted in direct accordance with his tastes. Thus, in an electoral system based on plurality voting, it is notorious that an individual who really favors a minor party candidate will frequently vote for the less undesirable of the major party candidates rather than 'throw away his vote.' Even in a case where it is possible to construct a procedure showing how to aggregate individual tastes into a consistent social preference pattern, there still remains the problem of devising rules of the game so that individuals will actually express their true tastes even when they are acting rationally. This problem is allied to the problem of constructing games of fair division, in which the rules are to be such that each individual, by playing rationally, will succeed in getting a preassigned fair share; in the case of two people and equal division, the game is very familiar one in which one player divides the total stock of goods into two parts, and the second player chooses which part he likes.[6]

Later we will note that these conditions rule out both strategic voting and what is generally called log-rolling.[7] I pointed this out in the article 'Is There a Paradox of Voting?' (*Journal of Theoretical Politics* 4(2): 225-230 (1992)). It is notable that this was sufficiently out of the orthodoxy so that the publishers put it under the heading 'Research Note' although they do not normally handle articles that way.

I only meet Ken Arrow at the national economic meeting and occasionally at other meetings. At the first meeting after this article was sent to him (it was before it was published although I had told him that it was to be published) he said that he had not answered because it was a very important matter and he had some unimportant matters that he wanted to finish off first. At the second meeting, a year later, he said that he had a counter example, but the counter example was complicated and he wanted a simple counter example. At the third meeting and after another year, he said that he was not going to reply.

Another important condition that Arrow does not mention is that the people actually have a complete preference ordering. If they are choosing among seven alternatives, for example as the Republican voters were in the primary process in 1996, they must have preferences over the entire set. Empirical evidence seems to indicate this would be rather rare.

Furthermore, these preferences have to be at least to some extent stable. If you find a person, let us say a Republican, who has a complete preference ordering over all of the candidates for the republican nomination, you will normally find that he has a pretty fixed idea as to which one is best and possibly which one is worst.

In the course of any lengthy conversation his attitude to the intermediate ones is apt to switch around. This is not a criticism, he just has not bothered to give it thorough consideration, and there is no obvious reason why he should. Nevertheless, it does make the formal proofs which will be dealt with mainly in this chapter rather irrelevant. How often would such situations occur? There have been a considerable number of studies of the possibility of intransitivity, ie. the situation we show in Figure 3.1, with different numbers of voters and different numbers of alternatives and the assumption that the preferences are completely independent of each other.[8] We will discover later in this book that the later assumption is probably not a very good one for the world and the voters in general do not have complete preference functions over a large number of alternatives. Still, in theory this is worth investigating.

It should be pointed out that if we deal not with the ordinary voters, but with the congressmen voting on the average bill, which is long enough so the congressman has not read it, there are an immense number of alternatives theoretically possible because each clause in the bill could be replaced by its opposite. Congressional procedures prevent this from happening, but the procedures which do prevent it from happening mean that very likely a superior alternative has been excluded.[9]

In any event this is clearly a case in which paradoxes can be measured by Monte Carlo methods.[10] The first such table is shown below as Table 3.1. It should be said that later work used more complicated and sophisticated computer routines, and produced larger tables. The general picture was not altered, and for sentimental reasons, I am using the original one.

It would appear that in any case in which we would have what I would call a reasonable collection of alternatives, not the ones that actually come out of the process at the final stage, but the total number of alternatives which are available, that intransitivity would be normal. The selection of the alternatives for the actual vote will be discussed in the next chapter. Unfortunately we know little about it.

Table 3.1: Percentage of cycles[11]

	3	5	7	9	11	13	15	17	19	21	23	25	27	29
3	5.7	7.8	8.4	8.9	8.5	7.3	7.4	8.4	8.0	8.9	9.1	9.7	11.1	11.1
4	10.7	14.6	15.9	15.6	15.1	14.7	15.5	17.3	16.9	17.2	16.4	18.0	18.6	17.4
5	15.4	18.3	21.5	23.0	25.1	22.4	25.3	23.7	23.9	24.8	25.4	24.3	24.0	21.1
6	20.1	25.5	25.8	28.4	29.4	28.1	29.8							
7	23.9	29.9	30.5	34.2	34.4	34.1	35.9							
8	27.7	32.5	36.7	37.8	38.6									
9	30.2	36.7	39.5	41.8	42.1									
10	32.4	40.8												
11	35.2				46.4				49.7					47.5
12														
13														
14														
15														
16														
17	46.4									62.6				
18														

Note: The vertical axis shows the number of issues, the horizontal axis the number of voters. The numbers in each cell show the average percentage of the numbers of cycles found in 1,000 cases.

There have been fewer studies of the type of paradox in which the removal or addition of a alternative far down the preference list changes the outcome. Further it is a little difficult to figure out exactly what these would show. This is because it is a little difficult to set up a system in which we have what I call reasonable elimination or addition of lower level preferences. In any event it appears this type of difficulty would be less likely granted independence of preferences and large number of alternatives than the kind which we have referred to as intransitivity. On the other hand, intransitivity appears to be simply a special case of the 'lack of independence of irrelevant alternatives' since the outcome is different depending on which particular alternative is left out.

We now turn to another area which was pioneered by Duncan Black.[12] He produced an example of a not terribly unlikely situation in which the intransitivity would not occur. Suppose that what we are dealing with is choices which can be arrayed along one axis. For example, how large an appropriation should be voted on this year for the Army.

Figure 3.4 shows a not unlikely situation, that is, each of the voters which we have only three to make the figure simple have some optimum and they become less and less happy as move away from the optimum in either direction. For the further use of this model it should be pointed out that it makes no great difference how high the optimum is drawn, or how rapidly it falls off. It is only that as you move away from it that it is necessary it fall off monotonously.

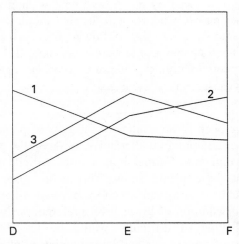

Figure 3.4: Single peak preferences

Under these circumstances there is no cycle and the middle preference will prevail. Sticking for the time being to this one dimension, it should be pointed out that this is a reasonably likely situation, although there are possibly differences. I am primarily interested in foreign affairs and it is frequently true my first preference is one extreme position, my second preference another, and compromise in the middle is worse than either. For example, in both Korea and Vietnam, I would have preferred either the policy of withdrawal, or the policy of fighting harder, to the policy which was actually accepted in both cases, which was to fight mildly for a long time.

Retrospectively, it would appear that the careers of Truman, Johnson and Nixon, would have been considerably happier had they considered my preference ordering, rather than the one they had. It should be said that their preference ordering fit the general public's views. It is clear that during both of these wars the presidential policy was in the middle with the people who wanted to fight harder balanced by the people who wanted to withdraw, and a group of people who thought that we should continue as is holding the middle. Thus they followed the median preference theorem, but the long-run results were depressing. If there had been a number of people with my preference orderings, as illustrated in Figure 3.5, cycles could have existed.

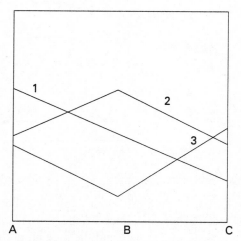

Figure 3.5: Cyclical preference

It seems likely that on a good many single issues the Black type single peak ordering of preferences is indeed what we observe in the real world. This requires that we choose along a one-issue issue dimension only. If we choose on two-issue dimensions, say the Army and Navy appropriations, then we need a two-dimensional diagram as in Figure 3.6.

Here we have three people with their optima in this two dimensional space. In each case, for simplicity, the degree to which they favor any alternative falls off gradually at the same rate in all directions so that their indifference curves are circles around their optimum.

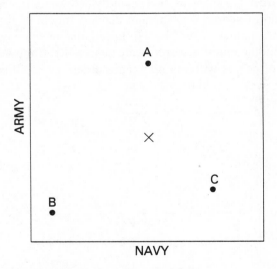

Figure 3.6: Army and Navy appropriations

For some reason if they are circles this is called 'Euclidian space'. This means that on either of the individual dimensions there is a single peak preference, and the median preference would win. Unfortunately, this is not true with the two-dimensional situation and I add that as the issues get more complicated so there are more than two dimensions the difficulty not only persists, it becomes worse. That this leads to cyclical majorities can be demonstrated easily and readily.

I have in Figure 3.6 drawn in the first preference of three different people which are in a rough triangle. Suppose 'X' is a proposal. It will be noted that if we draw indifference curves through X, as in Figure 3.7, it is obvious that the three intersect at point 'X' in such a way that there are three petal shaped spaces leading away from it.

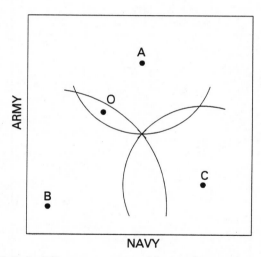

Figure 3.7: Indifference curves with two dimensions

Any point in any one of those petals can get a 2 to 1 majority against 'X'. If it is not obvious to the reader that this phenomena is apt to exist almost any where you put 'X' in the space, I suggest that you turn to the chapter in my *Toward a Mathematics of Politics*[13] entitled 'Pencil Exercises' where I demonstrate this with a large number of different locations.

This is a simple demonstration, lifted from Duncan Black,[14] that with more than one dimension, even if we have single peaked preferences along each of the dimensions, the outcome will be a cyclical majority. Since in the real world we normally have very many different interrelated issues which must be voted on and which can be presented in multi-dimensional space, cycles would appear to be normal and, hence, democracy essentially a generator of random outcomes.

This rather desperate situation led to research which made it seem even more desperate. Firstly Charles Plott demonstrated[15] that if you have a large number of persons voting in an area of this sort there would be a stable outcome only if there is one optimal preference of one voter which is central. Further, central is very tightly specified. Any straight line drawn through this central point must run through the same number of optima on either side of it.[16]

This is obviously an extremely tight restriction and was generally taken as indicating that the situation was hopeless.

Shortly after Plott produced his proof Ben Ward came up with a somewhat more desperate conclusion. He demonstrated that whoever controlled the agenda in this kind of space could, by setting up an appropriate chain of votes, move the outcome to practically any place he wished in the space. This led him to say that the United States had a concealed dictator and this concealed dictator was in fact the chairman of the Rules Committee of the House of Representatives.[17]

This was obviously a wildly unlikely theoretical development which we will talk about later, but it should be pointed out that a number of years afterwards a professor of political science at Harvard University, using another theory, tried to convince me that the chairman of each of the committees in the house was a concealed dictator for the particular part of the American government his committee dealt with.

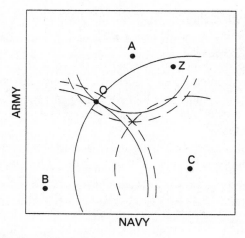

Figure 3.8: Successive votes

I repeat here Figure 3.8 with an O showing a possible outcome of a three person vote. I then produce another set of indifference curves through O. From these indifference curves we know Z can beat O and it is obviously farther from the center than O. By chains of this kind of voting one can get anywhere, but it requires a firm agenda control.

In a way, and purely temporarily, I rescued the field from this impasse. I demonstrated that if we have a large number of voters whose preferences are scattered over a space and their distribution is not too far from bell shaped, the situation is far from desperate.[18] If they are in a normal bell-shaped distribution or indeed in various distortions of such an arrangement, then the rules of order produce a reasonable solution.

What I showed was that under these circumstances if people are simply permitted to offer motions for vote, there would be a steady progress in toward the middle of the cloud of optima. This process would not lead to a point. After a while you would reach a small central area in which cycling could continue endlessly. Since most legislative bodies, and for that matter most direct voting bodies such as a town meeting, in fact do not permit continuous offering of amendments for tiny variations, when we reached this central area we would stop. The exact location of in which we stop will of course not be certain, but it would make relatively little difference. I did point out that if we did have some dictator that could arrange the votes, it would be possible even under these circumstances to move out almost any part of the figure you desire. I felt confident this never happened for a simple straightforward reason, movement a sizeable distance away from the center requires not only careful planning on the part on whomever sets up the agenda, but a long series of votes in which the majority and minority are divided by only one vote. Since we never see this happening in the real world I felt confident that it was not realistic, although theoretically it was possible.

For a short time this solution was orthodox, indeed Ben Ward came up to me at one of the meetings and said that he still did not believe it, but he could not find any flaw. Unfortunately, from the standpoint of the field McKelvey at this point produced a very general mathematical proof that one could reach any point in the space with appropriate agenda control.[19] He did not mention either Ward or myself in his original article. The illustrative examples that he gave had only a few voters, more than the three of figure six, but only a few and under such circumstances they do not look as wildly unrealistic as they would if he had, let us say, 435 voters. Further, it did not contradict my modification on Ward, but he did not mention the extreme restrictions on the movement away from the center if you have very many voters.

As far as I can see that is the present state of the theory about this subject. I myself feel that my contribution is the definitive one, but most of the people quote McKelvey and say that you can get anywhere in the space show no signs of being even interested in mine. I do agree that his is more mathematically elegant than mine.

All of this assumes Euclidian space, and indeed Euclidian space has been used in most of the work. There is no obvious reason to believe that this would be the norm. Suppose we go back to our two-dimensional figure, and assume that one of the dimensions is the army's appropriation, and another is the navy. The dimensions are marked off in dollar amounts.

There is no reason that these indifference curves around these points would have to be circles. Suppose that everybody thinks that it is very important that the army gets some tanks, and it would be nice for the navy to have some destroyers, but less important. This would lead to a set of ovals. Of course, since the ovals would have the same general shape for all of the voters, by a simple change in dimensions we get back to circles and the previous theorems would apply.

But suppose, and this seems not at all unlikely, there are some people who think it is very important that the army have more tanks, and that some destroyers to the navy would be nice, but not really essential, and there are some other people who feel that it is very important the navy have some destroyers, and that tanks for the army would be nice but not essential. We would then have ovals which are at right angles to each other, and the space would no longer be Euclidian.

As far as I know there has been no work on what comes out of this situation, but I have a hunch that my explanation that things would run in towards the middle, and not reach a point but stop because of the rules of order prohibiting small changes, to be the correct one. That is only a hunch, I haven't succeeded in providing even a rough demonstration. The closest I have come to it will be talked about later when we are dealing with log-rolling and 'a simple algebraic log-rolling model'.[20] There is a reason to make trades, and this does lead to a reasonably definite outcome, but unfortunately the definite outcome which it leads to is not a wonderfully desirable one.

I should perhaps turn to some really brilliant statistical work done by Mel Hinich and James Enelow.[21] They have examined real world politics in which two parties offer various policies, and have found there is a very strong tendency for the decisions in this multi-dimensional scheme to run towards the center, just as they would on Black's single-dimensional continuum. This would offer further reason why we don't observe so much instability.

I should say that I think the results are somewhat limited in theoretical structure. In the first place they are dealing with data drawn from a fairly strong two party system. If there are only two parties there is a strong pressure towards the middle as shown in my *Toward a Mathematics of Politics*, Chapter 4.[22] This comes from the fact that each party is trying to beat the other, and this means they must be near the other. If they are not near the center, at least one can gain by moving nearer to it.

In the multi-party system, such as we will discuss later when we return to proportional representation, the parties don't have this particular effect, but the coalitions that they produce in order to produce governments do have it. Further, in countries with proportional representation and cabinet government and nevertheless there is one party that tends to dominate; that party is normally drawn towards the center, although not so strongly.

To continue with this, a situation like that in the United Kingdom (which is rare, fortunately), where three parties with a central party which is relatively weak, there is considerable difference between the main two parties. This is because they don't have to get a majority vote, 40 to 45 percent is normally necessary, and they can let the middle votes go to the third party.

So far, I have been following a set of mathematical papers, which in my opinion are undeniably elegant and interesting, but require certain assumptions which do not fit real world voting. In the next chapter I will make the analysis more realistic.

One important reason for not believing that the mathematics that we have been going through are very important, is the simple fact that laws simply remain as they were for very long periods of time. If a law which is part of a cycle is passed, one would expect that as soon as the rules of order permit, which normally would be at the next session, another bill would be offered which, in the Condorcet cycle, could beat that one, and this process would continue indefinitely. We do not see that happening hence it seems likely that the kind of cyclical majority which would fit Arrow or McKelvey is in fact quite rare. This is on the whole fortunate both for democracy and for this book because in the rest of the book, we will make that assumption and deal with other problems of democracy.

---

1 At some times in the past, this was not true.

2 John F. Kennedy came very close if you accept the published figures. It was only the existence of some tiny third parties that prevented him from getting the majority of the published vote. If you do not accept them, if you are skeptical see my letter to the *New York Review of Books* and the reply. 'Did Nixon Beat Kennedy?' Letter to the editor, *The New York Review of Books* 35(17) (November 10, 1988): 53.

3 See *Condorcet, Foundations of Social Choice and Political Theory*, translated and edited by Iain McLean and Fiona Hewitt, Cheltenham: Edward Elgar, 1994.

4 See 'The Theory of Committees and Elections' and 'Voting with Complimentarily' written with R.A. Newing. These are to be brought out as a joint book by Kluwer with a forward by a Nobel Prize winner, Ronald Coase. This shows their importance even though they have been largely overlooked.

5 Arrow, Kenneth J. (1963). *Social Choice and Individual Values.* New York: John Wiley. 1963.

6 Arrow, Kenneth J. *Social Choice and Individual Values.* New York: John Wiley. (1963): 6–7, 11.

7   Both of these phenomena will be the subject of chapters later in this book.

8   The first one was Campbell and Tullock.

9   Granted the number of possible alternatives we could go beyond this and say that it is almost certain that a superior alternative has been excluded.

10 The first example was performed by Colin Campbell and myself. 'Computer Simulation of a Small Voting System.' *Economic Journal* 80 (March 1970): 97–104.

11 From Colin Campbell and Gordon Tullock 'A Measure of the Importance of Cyclical Majorities,' The Economic Journal LXXV (December 1965): 853-57.

12 Duncan Black first discovered the intransitivity problem by accident and in his autobiography (not yet in print) he says that it made him physically ill. I suspect the reason we do not have a great many ill in the present day world is that most people do not understand it, and turn to psychological defenses when it is explained to them.

13 University of Michigan Press 1967.

14 *Theory of Committees and Elections.* 2nd Edition. Kluwer Academic Publishers (forthcoming).

15 Plott, Charles R. 'A Notion of Equilibrium and its Possibility under Majority Rule.' *American Economic Review* 57 (September 1967): 787–806.

16 The number of optima could of course be zero on both sides of it since zero is an even number.

17 The last part of the sentence reports a personal conversation.

18 Tullock, Gordon. 'The General Irrelevance of the General Impossibility Theorem.' *Toward a Mathematics of Politics* University of Michigan Press, 1967.

19 McKelvey, Richard. 'General Conditions for Global Intrasitivities in Formal Voting Models.' *Econometrica* 47(5) (September 1979): 1085–112.

[20] 'A Simple Algebraic Logrolling Model.' *The American Economic Review* 60 (June 1970): 419–26. The individual preferences are all 3 or 5 dimensional, but they are ovals or flat disks depending upon the particular mathematical formation specified.

[21] See their two books both by Cambridge Press: *The Spatial Theory of Voting, An Introduction*, 1984 and *Advances in the Spatial Theory of Voting*, 1990. The latter is a collection of articles mainly by other authors.

[22] *Toward a Mathematics of Politics*, University of Michigan Press. Chapter 4 pp 59–61.

CHAPTER 4
Choice of Alternatives

Another reason why the Arrow and other mathematical problems do not fit the real voting procedure very well is because the alternatives which are to be chosen among by the voting process normally are pre-selected by some other method. We could, of course, have the voting process select the whole thing. All the possible alternatives could be put up using General Robert's rules and eventually through a series of binary choices we would reach an outcome.

The usual act of congress has at least 100 clauses all of which are objected to by at least one member of Congress and another several hundred clauses that were not in it but each of which were favored by at least one member of congress. They could all be offered and pairwise comparison with majority voting would produce an outcome. Unfortunately this system is absolutely guaranteed to produce cycles and the outcome would depend on the order in which the alternatives were presented. Further the one that finally came out would be certainly defeatable by one of the others. Fortunately, this is not the way it is done.

As an example of the kind thing that actually get into bills consider the following from *The Washington Post*:

Defense Appropriations Bill:
    Sen. John McCain (R-Ariz) sought unsuccessfully to set up a procedure

that would limit spending on 'unnecessary and unwarranted' projects, which he said accounted for at least $2 billion on the bill. He identified numerous items that had 'little to do with national defense,' including $1 million for brown snake control $477,000 to integrate schools at Fort Leavenworth, Kansas, and $2 million for a National Automotive Center.

Under McCain's amendment, the secretary of defense would have to certify that such items fulfill a military requirement and meet other criteria. It was defeated on a voice vote.[1]

Anyone who pays any attention to congressional acts quickly realizes that similar irrelevancies are to found in almost every bill. Stockman refers to the 'federal soup kitchen' in which small items are added to bills in order to attract votes.

Stockman discusses this process a number of times in his book.[2] 'In the Congress, the "soup kitchen" is what you throw open in the last hours before a vote to get people off the fence. At this point, democracy becomes not a discussion of the ideals of Jefferson or the vision of Madison. It becomes a $200,000 feasibility study of a water project; the appointment of a regional director of the Farmers' Home Administration in western Montana.'[3]

But this is not the only item. Consider the question of what bills are presented to begin with, not just to all the changes to buy votes. Take a specific problem. During the first two years of the Clinton administration the Democrats had control of both houses of Congress. The subject of a minimum wage raise was never even mentioned anywhere in the Congress or by the President or his aides. In the second two years of Clinton's presidency the Republicans had control of both the house and the senate. The President and the Democratic minority in these two houses immediately began pushing vigorously for the increase in the minimum wage.

Nothing in the real world had changed that made the minimum wage more important then than before, but the political calculus had changed. They were able by this method to severely embarrass the republicans and force through the minimum wage to increase the total unemployment, etc., for teenagers. To repeat, the current public choice literature does not give a good explanation of how these kind of things work except by a general reference to politics.

I frankly admit that this chapter is not going to clear up the problem but it will at least point out that we need to work on it and offer some hints as the direction which the research should go.

Let me give another example. Terry B. Kinney, Jr., a high official in the Department of Agriculture had decided to make certain economies in the running of the department of agriculture and the following account shows the difficulty.

> In one simple plan we proposed to move three bee researchers from Wyoming to Texas to expand research on the African bee, migrating rapidly north from Mexico. We would use funds saved from the bee research to conduct studies to help solve a serious soil erosion problem in Wyoming. Over long months we developed every detail of the move. We had even obtained the cooperation of university and state officials and important congressmen and senators. Then came a phone call passed from the secretary and on to me: "Don't move the bee research."
>
> Two days later came another telephone message: "Proceed with the soil erosion project."
>
> "Where will we get the money?" I asked.
>
> "Find it somewhere," I was told.
>
> What had happened? The president needed votes for his MX Missile Program. The bee and the soil erosion programs were two of the price tags Senator Malcolm Wallop (R-Wyo.) put on his vote. (Agency heads and their staffs have extensive and reliable grapevines by which they learn such things.)[4]

These are simple examples and we could find many more if we wished. For an unusually extreme case:

> A final accident of the reconciliation battle tells the lasting story. On June 26, 1981, Rita Seymour and her telephone number (255-4848) were voted into law by an amuck House of Representatives. Ms. Seymour was only a low-level Congressional Budget Office staffer. But in frantically trying to add up the spending-cut numbers the brawling Representatives were about to enact, her name and number got scribbled on the page margin of the

reconciliation bill. So she got mistakenly enacted along with the budget figures".[5]

For further examples, just read the newspaper.[6] You will find that most bills go through various committees and differences between the two houses almost always turn up. It may be delayed for a lengthy time for a number of changes. The final version very frequently has not been read in its entirety by anybody.

The discussion of bills in the newspapers normally turns around what we might call the more important provisions and I, of course, will not deny that this is sensible. Although these important provisions are indeed important, there will be a vast volume of minor provisions in the bill many of which are known only to a few congressmen and in some cases only to the legislative assistants of some individual congressmen. The volume of bills passed by Congress each year is clearly too long for any congressmen, no matter how devoted to work, to actually read all of them let along give them careful consideration.

Discussions of this, including Stockman's, are written in a tone of considerable indignation. Here we are interested not in exhibiting emotions about it but discussing or at least investigating how it is done. Certainly it is not true that any congressman can get anything he wishes added into any bill. There must be some kind of rationing process. I cannot produce a genuine formal account of this, although a formal account which resembles it will in fact be presented a little later in the chapters on log-rolling.

But there is another issue which is original bills themselves and the parts of them which are indeed relevant to the particular subject. In other words, that bill on defense which included the protection of snakes also had an amendment offered to increase the number of marine corp generals. It was voted down but clearly it was relevant.

To discuss this, let us begin with a very simple example. My sister lives in Eldora, Iowa a little town of 3,300 population on the

Iowa River and there are a number of other small towns in the vicinity. Some time ago various people in these towns decided it would be a good idea to create the Iowa River Greenbelt as a conservation measure.

I do not know how they reached this conclusion. Presumably a few people thought it was a good idea and told others who then agreed. In any event, they were able to get the little towns to make, normally not very great, efforts to produce something in the way of a Greenbelt. Efforts to get the federal government and the state government involved were, on the whole, unsuccessful. Recently I have noticed that although people still sometimes talk about the Greenbelt, interest in it seems to have fallen off.

This is a very tiny example but the same thing will be found if you read almost any account of the details of government functioning. Indeed, if you read accounts of intellectual history in which the government is totally left out, subjects suddenly pop up, are important for a while, and then disappear. As far as I know we have no explanation for this phenomenon although I cannot imagine that many of my readers will be surprised by it. Presumably most of them can think of many examples on their own.

At a more interesting level, during the time that I was preparing this particular chapter the idea of giving the District of Columbia very special tax treatment with the intent of getting people to move back into it developed. In just a few days lengthy proposals to this effect were set out. Interestingly enough the representative of the District of Columbia in congress[7] and Newt Gingrich were highly in favor, and so, for that matter, were leading republicans in the Senate. Granted that the voters of the District of Columbia are probably at least 80 percent democrat it is astonishing that any republicans at all were involved.

It should be pointed out that a proposal that the taxes be lowered in the District of Columbia is hardly likely to be popular with the constituents of congressmen from Iowa. At the time this is being dictated the idea seems to be dropping out and one of the reasons that it is dropping out is that various constituents have noticed that the congressmen themselves live in the District of Columbia and hence, think that it is an effort to get a reduction for them.

Indeed, the paper on the day in which I am actually dictating this chapter suddenly said that it looked like it would be through next year instead of immediately. I predict that in two more weeks the idea will have disappeared completely.[8] To repeat what I have been emphasizing here, we have no real theory to explain this.

I want to take up another important issue that caused a great deal of difficulty. The decision that we should ban alcoholic beverage consumption by an amendment to the Constitution, just simply arose. The decision that we should repeal the amendment and permit alcoholic beverage consumption also is one that simply rose up. In both cases, of course, there were active movements backing the change, but why did these movements back these changes instead of some others.

While we are on the subject of drugs, the attitude towards other drugs, the so-called hard drugs or some of the softer drugs like LSD and marijuana, goes up and down and the government normally takes action in terms of how strong public opinion is at the moment. There is no evidence that attempts to manipulate public opinion were responsible.

All of this appears to be something which we should turn to psychology or perhaps intellectual history to explain, and frankly I do not think we have a good explanation at the moment. It is very important if we are talking about voting because votes are characteristically cast on issues that have been selected either by simply coming up, as these do, or as a result of complicated internal activity in congress in which minor things are added on. There are also, of course, certain bills that have to be passed regularly, the budget bills are an example which do not depend upon public enthusiasm, but it is also true the development or failure of public enthusiasm has a good deal to do with when such bills are presented.

All of this may impress the readers as having nothing to do with voting and, in fact, it does not. It does, however, draw a line around voting. Normally when we get to the actual voting process and consider problems that are raised by the mathematics of voting when there are many alternatives, most of the alternatives have already disappeared. Very commonly in the House of Representatives or the House of Commons there are literally only two alternatives, shall we or shall we not pass a given bill. Details of the bill, which have of course a great deal to do with whether it will pass have been already established by other methods.

In general, although not entirely, it is very hard to amend bills on the floor of congress. It is even hard to amend bills before the city council of Tucson. Clearly in both of these cases, there are an immense number of minor changes, and even some fairly major ones, which would be favored by some people and which they would like to have put before the legislature to vote on. They are not voted on.

I am not going to devote a great deal of attention here to how this is done. The point is simply that the fact that a large proportion of the active work in any legislative body is done by some method other than general votes means that the mathematical problems which we mentioned in the last chapter are in general of less importance. Those problems rise, in general, only if there are a number of alternatives. If you simply have an up or down yes of no vote on a given bill there is no significant problem. If you have only a couple of amendments each of which, once again, faces an up or down vote there are some problems but not many. In general then the mathematical problems which we have been talking about are not of vast importance.

If we consider a legislature, and we make our previous simplifying assumptions, we find that each legislature has a long list of things that he would like, and another list of things which he is opposed to, and probably ones which he does not care for very much. The situation is much that of a housewife going out to shop with a limited budget. He then begins bargaining with his fellow congressmen but not facing a fixed set of prices as the housewife would.

In a way he is in an oriental souk rather than in an American mall. Obviously, he tries to make the best general deal that he can. The congressmen have different levels of skill, fewer or more connections, and different positions in the internal structure of congress.

In spite of all these things, the individual congressman presumably makes the best deal that he can, and in general the outcome is not voted on in such a way as to permit the cyclical majority or the lack of independence of alternatives that we have previously discussed.

It is true that if a new alternative is introduced in the middle of a discussion this may mean that the representative will want to revise some of the bids. Basically, as in the case of the housewife, the problems that Arrow mentioned do not occur because each individual choice is accompanied by a price.

If all of the alternatives that any individual congressman favored were introduced as amendments those would have literally hundreds of such amendments and would take an immense time to vote on, and almost certainly would be a case in which the outcome was not a Condorcet choice. Indeed, it would be on the whole unlikely that there was a Condorcet choice in such a set. In the congressman's case, the price takes the form of a vote on something else. As a result there is no ordering of the alternatives first to last because some pair of alternatives at lower prices may replace a single alternative if this bargaining structure is such that it is possible.

I do not want to argue that the system works perfectly. Anybody who has had any experience or has been reading accounts of this realizes quickly that it does not work at all perfectly. Still it is immune to what we might call the Arrow problem. Arrow's basic conditions quoted above simply do not apply.

This is a different picture from the standard one. In the first place, the arguments that do exist for simple majority voting are based on the assumption that most projects are what we might call general benefit or general injury. There is no doubt that there are such things and that congressmen to some extent cast votes in terms of them. Take the military appropriations. Everybody in Congress is interested in these in terms of what we may call the well-being of the United States. This applies both to strict anti-military pacifists and to those who feel that it is important that we have a powerful army. This feeling will have major influence on their voting. On the other hand, there is no doubt, as anyone who has looked at the proceedings will realize, that all of the congressmen are interested in various special parts of it. A pacifist may be absolutely convinced that the military base in his district should be kept open, perhaps get a larger appropriation. This is only one example of this kind of thing. In dealing with the actual discussion one frequently gets the idea that congressmen are less interested in the general policy than the specific. This is not in fact true. It is simply that the specific details necessarily involve a great deal more discussion.

Even though the congressmen with respect to the military budget are primarily motivated by their views of the general good, it should be pointed out that it can be traded against other things where other general goods are involved. A firm environmentalist may be wiling to sacrifice certain environmental goals if he feels the money is really needed for defense, and of course vice versa.

In most of the areas these details are such that they have a benefit for one or a few congressmen, and a general detriment to the others where taxes are to be collected to pay for them. This is not a case in which one could argue that simple majority voting which gives the outcome to the majority is sensible. The cost to the losers for the whole set is considerably greater than the benefit to the winners. This was the reason why the *Calculus of Consent*, and earlier[9] work suggested the desirability of more than majority voting.

The people who objected to this, and argued strongly for majority voting, for example Douglas Rae,[10] never object to the unanimity in juries, two thirds majorities in the senate if there is significant opposition, the complicated amendment procedure of our constitution, and last but not least, the combination of a two house legislature, and a presidential veto which involves effectively more than the majority. Clearly majority voting is for them a slogan, and is not part of their real reasoning.

We see that the actual voting procedure in congress is not a choice between direct alternatives but a complex bargaining process in which alternatives appear and disappear, in which congressmen may vote for things that they detest because they have been adequately paid. There is no reason we should object to this but we should realize that is what goes on, and not use the slogans of the high school civics course.

The result of all of this is that most formal voting is made on a simple up or down two-sided choice in which event the Arrow theorem does not apply. The putting together of the thing that they vote on is done by various committees, individual influence, etc. and we do not fully understand this although there is a vast literature in the political science field which describes various specific examples.

I begin with one example that occurred in Tucson when I first arrived. Arizona is one of these states where cities have bond issue elections and the city fathers had made up a complex package of improvements on schools, parks, and roads, and submitted this as a bond issue to the citizens of the city. It was voted down. Note that there are only two alternatives, either do it or not do it, hence the Arrow theorem did not apply.

The city fathers came to the conclusion that the problem was that they did not have enough in their program for southeast

Tucson. They accordingly made up another bundle which had more for southeast Tucson and in fact more for various other people at a higher tax cost, put that to election, and it won. Once again, a two-choice election.

I believe, however, and obviously I can not prove this, that if the first program would have been put against the second one it would in fact have beaten the other. In other words, there was a cycle. Program A was thought to be inferior by a majority of the voters to doing nothing. Program B was thought to be better by a majority of the voters than doing nothing. Program A was also thought by a majority of the voters to be better than Program B.

The same phenomenon is one of the basic reasons that bills passed by congress do not get revoked. Suppose that Stockman has bought enough votes for his budget by providing a very large bit of boodle for various people. Once it is passed, he proposes[11] that a whole collection of these minor things be thrown out. If he is selected the minor things properly, they are things that a clear majority of the legislature would rather not have if voted on one by one.

The problem here is firstly, if he began doing that, people would stop selling their votes to him. If you are engaged in illegal activity, like, for example, currency black-marketing, it is very important that you have a good credit rating because there is no legal enforcement of the agreement. The same is true with log-rolling.

The black market is a particularly clear cut case and has an amusing example. When *Dr. Zhivago* first came out, it was published in western countries and not in Russia. The western publishers, many of them in any event, said that they would be delight to pay Pasternak, or his wife, royalties, but it would be difficult. Shortly after this, a Russian, whom Mrs. Pasternak had never seen before in her life, walked into her apartment and handed her a large number of rubles without even giving her his name.

This was the black market functioning with perfect credit efficiency. Unfortunately, she talked about it.

The same is true with these bargains we are now talking about. It seems likely that if Stockman had somehow gotten the thing up for a vote, a large number of people would have voted in favor of things that they really opposed because they knew it was necessary to do so to keep their credit for future bargains. The details of this will be taken up later when we turn to formal log-rolling.

There is a possibility of getting a direct public vote in various places. California, Arizona, and Switzerland are examples, but you have to have a sizeable number of names on the petition. In the case of Tucson, there were no groups of people who felt strongly enough in favor enough of Alternative *A* as opposed to Alternative B to organize such a petition. It was therefore never voted on.

Countries like Switzerland and states like California where there are a lot of such petitions and a lot of such proposals are interesting in that the real vital part of the whole thing is the making up of the proposal. I do not want to exaggerate here. Both in making up these proposals and in making up this kind of bargain which Stockman described so well, the desire of getting through the final hurdle of the voting process with a majority is always there. Indeed in those states where this process is required for constitutional amendments and where the constitutional amendment requires a two-thirds majority, you have to make it up with the intent of getting a two-thirds majority.

As far as I know, the actual process of putting these things together with various clauses being modified, language changed, etc. in order to get the appropriate number of votes is pretty much unrecorded. There is one exception to this, the Constitutional convention itself where the matters were recorded reasonably completely by Madison. The specific issue of getting a two-thirds majority, earlier mentioned, and the constitution, as adopted, was simply a blown up version of the constitutions used by most of the states for their own affairs.

It is notable at the very end General Washington suggested that the number of votes necessary to set up a congressional district be lowered which would mean there would be more congressmen. It is clear that he did this because he thought that it would help in getting it adopted. Insofar as I know this is the only clear-cut case of adjustment for the need to get a large majority.

In many ways, this building up of the proposal is the most important thing that happens and it is unfortunate that although we have a good general idea of how this is done, these ideas are only general. Our formal discussion of log-rolling will help to illuminate these issues.

All of this may sound like an attack on democracy. It is certainly an indication that democracy does not work in an ideal way. The question, however, is what are the alternatives. Further, the process of getting a hereditary king or a dictator to adopt some policy runs along much the same lines. There is the same bundling in of essentially irrelevant issues in order to get support, not of course voting support, but support in the court.[12] The absence of this kind of maneuvering is not something we should use as a criteria of government because it will be used in all of them. The details vary but the general principles do not.

---

[1] *Washington Post*, July 18, 1996, pg. A4.

[2] Stockman, David. *The Triumph of Politics* (New York: Harper & Row, 1986).

[3] Stockman, David *The Triumph of Politics* (New York: Harper & Row, 1986): 221.

[4] Kinney, Terry B. 'The Reason of the Clerks' *Reason* 28(6) (August 1996): 30. The magazine *Reason* is generally speaking violently opposed to the bureaucracy and most bureaucrats are in face against cutting the budget although they do not say so. Thus, the fact that this article ran in *Reason*

is quite astonishing. Both parties to this transaction are talking against interest.

5   Stockman, op. cit. p. 277.

6   At the time of writing, the British Conservative government had lost its nominal majority when a member surrendered the whip because the government had not provided a 2-hour emergency room in his district.

7   She has no vote but is influential.

8   The prediction was verified.

9   Tullock, Gordon. 'Problemi del voto a maggioranza.' Francesco Forte and Gianfranco Mossetto eds. *Economia del Benessere e Democrazia* (Milano: Franco Angeli Editore 1973): 459–71.

10 Tullock, Gordon. 'Comment on Rae's "The Limit of Consensual Decision",' *American Political Science Review* 69 (4) (December 1975): 1295–97.

11 It might be very difficult for him to get any member of Congress to actually put the proposal in the hopper.

12 My discussion of this and many other aspect of an absolute monarchy's court by a man who knew it very well, see *A Practical Guide for Ambitious Politicians*, Anonymous, Edited by Gordon Tullock, University of South Carolina press, Columbia, South Carolina, 1961. This is a very popular guide for courtiers written long ago.

CHAPTER 5
Simple Vote Trades

This chapter will further loosen the tight requirements of formal mathematical theory by pointing out that under a number of circumstances people do not vote according to their strict preferences. This, as the quotation from Kenneth Arrow in Chapter 3 indicates, takes the discussion even further out of the domain of the strict Arrow proof or my somewhat milder proof. As we proceed through the book, we shall move more and more from the strict mathematical theory of voting as developed by Arrow to a more realistic theory of democracy.

I should say that Arrow's proof when it was published puzzled a number of people because it is mathematically difficult, but substantially no one actually objected to his conditions. There was some criticism of the particular requirement that the voting procedure should not 'lack independence, of irrelevant or alternatives'. I think this criticism arose to a large extent because most people had never thought of this particular problem until they read his proof. Most political scientists had been engaging in empirical research, but the theoretical structure they imposed on it did not have much rigor.

The reader will recall the quotation of Arrow in the first chapter and his statement that people might vote against their preferences because they have been given something in return. In general, as I mentioned in the last chapter, cash payments are illegal and although there does not seem to be much data on it, I do not think that they are very important in the United States at the moment. The other kind of gift, however, a log-rolling trade, dominates all of our actual legislation. Most of these trades are made by professionals.

One of the advantages, from the student's standpoint, of the American legislatures as opposed to most European ones is that these trades are much more open and hence are easier to study here than they are in most countries. Still, there isn't much in the way of formal statistics on it and people who do empirical work have to use indirect approaches.

As an example, Groseclose in his article 'The Market for Favors and Votes' depends on number of not such wonderful sources.[1] Still, we are better off than most students of European parliaments. A former student holds a high position in the Dutch equivalent of the Office of Management and Budget told me that the only difference between the Dutch parliament and the American Congress was that all the negotiations were strictly secret in the Netherlands.

Having said that this is the way that the government actually works, I am going to start with some negotiations of this sort that are not very close to our modern Congress simply because it is always easier to start with a simple model and then complicate it. The model is the one that I introduced many years ago in an article in an article entitled 'Problems of Majority Voting.'[2]

In this model we have about one hundred farmers who live on a number of lanes off a main road, the main road being maintained by the higher authorities and the farmers collectively responsible for the lanes. About five live on each lane and they make decisions which lanes to repair and how well by majority vote among the hundred. Repair costs are taxed on the farmers equally. Since all of the roads deteriorate with use, such repairs are needed from time to time.

There are various ways individual farmers could use their votes. One would be always to vote for the repair of their own lane and never to vote for the repair of others, since there will be general taxation and the repair of the other lanes will benefit a given farmer substantially less than its tax cost. This of course would lead to no roads being repaired.

Another is what I call the Kantian method; each farmer has an idea as to how badly a road must deteriorate before it is repaired. When any road, including the farmer's own lane, deteriorates to the point where repairs are put to vote, he will evaluate the lane and if it has deteriorated far enough so that by his general standard it should be repaired he will vote for repairing it, if not he will vote against it.

If farmers used this particular method then we would have the decisions on repairing roads would fit the single peak preference curves of the last chapter. Each farmer would have a ideal degree of road repairing on a single dimension as in the figure below and roads would be repaired when in bad enough condition so that the median voter, M, thought that they should be repaired.

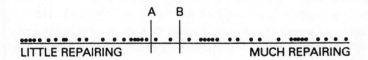

Figure 5.1: Kantian voters

Suppose A, however, follows another rule. He always votes for repairing his own road and never votes for repairing any of the others. The result of this is that his road would be repaired somewhat better than it was before and his total tax bill would be somewhat lower because other farm roads would not be repaired quite as quickly as before he changed his voting rule. It is likely that many farmers would adopt this rule and the people that followed the Kantian procedure would gradually find that their roads were in worse and worse condition and that their tax bill did not decline proportionately.

Needless to say, discussions of something similar to my Kantian rule are frequently found in the literature and it is quite possible that on many areas of no great importance to the individual voter that is the way people do vote. In general the kantian rule is dominated by others for most individuals.

The basic other means that we deal with here is bargaining, called log-rolling in this context. The farmers on lane *A* go around to the farmers on ten other lanes and offer, that if these farmers will vote for repairing the road *A*, they will vote for repairing the other roads. Assume that their proposed partners agree and hence road *A* is repaired. The five persons on lane *B*, having voted for repair of *A*, and thus having votes of the residents of lane *A* in their pockets go around and bargain with voters on nine other roads to vote for *B*.

Note that there is no reason why the people voting for the repair of road *B* should except for those on lane *B* and lane *A*, be the same as those who voted for the repair of road *A*. We can assume that the process continues until all of the roads are repaired. The reader may have wondered how we know that they all would be repaired, and we do not, but that particular subject will be put aside until a little later.

We have not reached the Kantian outcome. Each of the individuals entering into a bargain with voters on other roads has to take into account the cost of the repairing of eleven roads, not the cost of the repairing of all roads. Under the circumstances they will keep their road repaired at a higher level than is actually optimal because the cost to them is only a little over half of the actual cost of repairing it. The rest of the cost will be borne by the minority not included in the individual bargains.

Note that this is a very simple model at the moment, but it still gives the basic argument for feeling that something more than a simple majority is desirable. For example, if we required unanimous consent for any road repair, temporarily ignoring bargaining problems, it is clear that that rule would give you road repairing at the optimal level since all of the voters have to contrast repairs on their road with their taxes over the entire set. Of course, to repeat this is not a very practical rule.

However, we do not have to talk about unanimous consent except for theoretical reasons. Suppose that we required a two-thirds majority instead of a simple majority.[3] Each voter would take into the account two-thirds of the actual cost of repairing the roads as the coalition would have to pay two-thirds of it. Hence the amount of the repairs of the roads would be more efficient than under simple majority voting.

As a sort of contrast to our unrealistic unanimous consent above we could have a rule that whenever the voters on one road wish to have it repaired it is indeed immediately repaired at the cost to the entire voting group. This would obviously lead to a vast over investment of road repair as each group would be paying only one-twentieth of the cost of repairing their road. Like the unanimity criteria it is not something that we are likely to encounter in the real world.

Suppose that among the road voters there is one with considerable entrepreneurial ability and he decides that he can do better. He proposes to set up a permanent coalition of people who live on eleven roads and they will vote to have their roads repaired up to the level desired when they pay half of the cost and will not waste money on repairing the other nine lanes. From the standpoint of the members of this new coalition it is better than the previous status quo.

In general coalitions of this sort are radically unstable. The reason that they are unstable is that the other nine roads can approach two members of this cartel and offer them very much better road repair in return for abandoning the cartel and joining their group.

The cartel has no punishment for this because it now no longer has the majority of the voters. The defectors gain, but further defections are likely so their gains are impermanent. Such cartels are unstable, each being dominated by several other potential cartels. Here we have a clear example of the rotating majority.

Let us discuss an optimal voting rule for these people. Firstly, as we pointed out, the one person rule and the unanimity rule are not likely to work but that does not seem to be any great argument for a simple majority. There are two costs here, one of which is the cost of having an inefficient level of road repair and the other is, of course, the tax.

Let us confine ourselves to a very simple model. In Figure 5.2 we have on the left the situation where any individual can simply order his road repaired at the cost of the community. As we move to the right more and more people are required to agree, finally at the right end roads can only be repaired by unanimity.

We would anticipate that the individual order system would inflict very great costs on the voters since although their own road would be repaired to a superb level they would be paying the cost of other people's roads too. As the number of people required to agree increased, both the level of repair of their road and the amount they have to pay to repair other roads would decline.

The rate at which it would decline in Figure 5.2 is put in purely from theoretical considerations, there is no empirical work on it that I know of. I feel some confidence that it is at least approximately correct, however, because when I first introduced the figure above drawn with this decline, no one complained. It has not been objected to since then even though the figure itself has been put in a number of text books and many political scientists offer general objections to the conclusions I draw, but they never object to the shape of this curve.

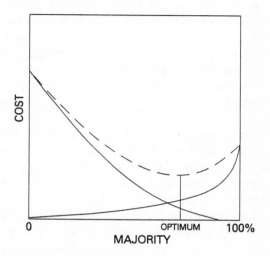

Figure 5.2: Optimal majority

But while this leads to the optimal level of road repair at the unanimous requirement there is another problem here which is the bargaining cost. There is no bargaining cost if I can simply order the roads repaired, if I have to get agreement with one other person so that we have the two-person rule, there would be some bargaining cost, and as the number of people required to agree goes up the total bargaining cost would rise. This is shown by the second line on the figure. Note there are two regimes here. In the early phase of the bargaining, that is numbers up to, let us say, 80 percent it is just that, bargaining. You have to put together a bundle of road repair projects that at least 80 percent of the population will gain from, and we would anticipate for the reasons that we have given before that as a matter of fact there would be many such overlapping bargains.

When we begin getting up close to unanimity, however, the situation changes. At this point individuals can feel that their refusal to go along raises the real chance that the whole bargain will be lost. They can thus make efforts to acquire for themselves by way of improved road repair and low taxes the entire or a very large part of the benefit that the entire community gets from such road repair. Thus we would anticipate that the line would have the shape that I have shown, gradually rising and then very steep at the end. This would of course indicate why we so rarely require unanimity.[4]

We now sum these two lines as is shown in the figure and the low point is the point at which the most efficient road repair will be carried out. The cost of investment and bargaining of taxes and of not having your roads repaired just exactly the way you would like are all incorporated there.

There is no reason why this low point should be at the 50 percent level and indeed substantially nobody ever argues that it is.[5] Effectively all practical discussions of this assume more than majority voting as the low point with the result that they are assumed to imply more than a majority.

This line of argument in effect says that we must do our best to include everyone or as close to it as is feasible into the electoral bargain. If we do not, the majority of whatever the number is can, and no doubt will, inflict cost on the minority.

This has been objected to with great vigor by conventional political scientists. But their normal argument consists, circularly, in demonstrating that any rule other than majority voting reaches a different conclusion than majority voting. As a criticism this requires an assumption that majority voting is right.

If we make the assumption that anything except majority is wrong we should for example immediately revise the jury system. Further the filibuster rule in the senate, the presidential veto, and the requirement of reinforced majorities for constitutional amendments all would be wrong. Even the two house legislature with the two houses being elected differently offends again majority voting since it is a stiffer requirement than majority in one house. These conclusions are never drawn by the people who object to the argument given above. What they actually do invariably is find some simple yes/no decision by a single voting body. To take one example used in several political science articles (some time ago), suppose the people in a railroad car take a vote on whether smoking is to be permitted or not.[6] If we assume that the persons are about equally distributed in terms of intensity, majority voting would be a good idea. Clearly if everybody is either in favor of smoking or against smoking and all of them will be equally displeased if they do not get their will then you minimize the amount of displeasure in the society by majority voting.

This of course requires that the intensity of feelings be evenly balanced, about as much intensity on one side as the other. If we have some people in the car who feel that another's smoking actually endangers their life, and there are lots of such people around these days, they would presumably feel much more intensely about it than would the people who want to smoke. Thus the rule would not be optimal, and would not minimize felt dissatisfaction.

It may seem here that I am setting up a straw man although I assure you that I have run into this argument many times, but I believe that the actual situation is that most Americans simply believe majority voting is the right thing to do except in all of the cases in which by our custom we do not do it. To repeat (again) the general category, majority voting is intended to take in unanimous voting in juries, two-thirds vote in both Houses to overcome a presidential veto, etc. It is in other words, not a statement about the desirability of the majority vote, but a statement that a whole wide variety of different rules that we are accustomed to should be retained.

It is not clearly true that this is an error. A certain amount of structural or theoretical conservatism is usually a good idea. What now exists has some reason behind it and should be overturned only if there are pretty good reasons against it. In fact we thought that our argument in _The Calculus of Consent_, which I have given above, provided a considerable justification for the existing rules.

So far we have mainly been talking about a very simple model, although I have deviated into talking about the actual American constitution. In the next chapter we will have a more complex model, but let me close this chapter by dealing with an objection that may very well have occurred to the reader. What could be done is simply appoint an engineer for all of these roads, and have the individual voters vote on the general level of repair, in which event we would be back at the Kantian system and then the engineer would simply make the decisions in terms of that general level. Anyone who has had any serious dealings with civil servants would realize that this system would not work out perfectly, but it probably would work out reasonably well.

There are two reasons why, in all probability, it would not be feasible. The first of these is that after the engineer had made decisions on all roads a coalition of 51 voters could raise the amount on their road. In order to prevent this it would be necessary to have some kind of constitutional limitation under which they were not permitted to vote to change the administered decision. Constitutions can be changed, usually by reinforced majority so this method gets us back to requiring more than a majority. Whether it is a better way of depending on more than a majority voting than given above, I will leave to the reader.

The second reason is that it is impractical in most real world cases where this kind of political bargaining goes on. As a general rule political bargaining does not deal with a set of more or less identical projects benefiting a set of small groups. More commonly the projects differ immensely. To take an extreme example, which I find amusing, Congressman Udall obtained the Central Arizona

Project in Arizona[7] in part by agreeing that he would always vote against any development in Alaska. Thus he got a bunch of environmental votes even though the project itself is the kind of thing environmentalists normally object to.

It is hard to see how we could have an expert be given a standard set of instructions to deal with this kind of trade. Udall of course also voted in general for the agricultural program which inflicted very large costs on the consumers of agricultural products in order to give modest gains to farmers, most of whom were not in Udall's district.

But we could easily go on. There were projects actually completed to make Tulsa a deep water port and to construct what amounts to a parallel Mississippi connecting the Ohio with the gulf. At the time of writing the mayor of New York is attempting to spend an immense amount of money to construct a new stadium for one of the New York baseball teams. In other words the kinds of trades that we have dealt with here are in general trades between things for which it is not possible to set up a simple rule which the voters could vote on and then have experts apply that rule.

If we go back into the early history of the United States, there were, for the federal government, only a few projects of this sort. There were tariffs, naval and military bases, both on a small scale and what was called development, which mainly meant building canals.[8] We could argue with respect to the tariffs and the developments that some kind of civil servant judgments could have been made with the basic rule voted upon, but that is not what happened. It is true that at various times general policies of lowering tariffs were adopted but these were always reversed. Possibly this unfortunate history is now ending.

The general picture here is that trading between various political projects, carried on by various political entrepreneurs is the basic way in which most democracies function. It leads to a very large number of projects which benefit small areas at a very general cost. It should be pointed out that it is by no means obvious that all of these projects would fail cost benefit tests as is also true of the roads in my model.

Nevertheless, many of them certainly do. The Central Arizona Project mentioned above is almost unique among government projects in that the City of Tucson is actually worse off as a result of vast amount of monies spent by the taxpayers in the rest of the country, than if it would be had they not spent the money at all. As far as I know there are no other examples. Water projects in the west are commonly not worth what they cost, but I think we[9] are the only one that can actually claim we have a project which had a negative pay-off.

All of these subjects will be dealt with in much greater detail in Chapter 6, to which I hope the reader will now turn.

---

[1] *Economic Inquiry*, April 1996, Tim Groseclose pp. 320-40.

[2] *Journal of Political Economy* 67 (December 1959): 571-79.

[3] In a good many cases in the United States there is a direct popular vote on bond issues for various local improvements. It is not particularly uncommon for these bond issues to require more than the majority vote to pass.

[4] The unanimous jury appears just to be a hangover from medieval times.

[5] There is a confused argument in Mueller's *Public Choice* on this point. He assumes that the vote if we use less that the majority rule could then be beaten by another less than majority not to repair the road. In this particular situation that is of course impossible because we are simply voting on whether to repair and it requires 40 percent. If 59 percent object to the road being repaired it would nevertheless be repaired. It is however as far as I know very, very rare that anyone suggests less than majority rules for anything except things like the United States presidential election. Where it is

used there have to be more than two candidates and the initial vote is final.

Lincoln, Wilson, and Clinton were all elected by markedly less that the majority of the popular vote because there were more than two candidates. Kennedy was elected on slightly less than the majority and in fact probably had fewer votes than Nixon.

See my 'Did Nixon beat Kennedy?' and the 'response' Letters to the Editor, *The New York Review of Books* 35(17) (Nov. 10, 1988): p. 53.

6 This was back in the days they could conceivably vote on this issue; there was no law.

7 He had the assistance of a number of other people from Arizona.

8 Jefferson, and his Secretary-Treasurer had an almost insane project to build no less than 5 canals over the Appalachian mountains. They spent a lot of money, and never succeeded in coming close to completion.

9 I live in Tucson.

CHAPTER 6
Direct Voting with Log-Rolling

When Buchanan and I first began to work on *The Calculus of Consent*[1] I looked though the index of a number of elementary texts in political science and discovered that most of them did not even have log-rolling listed. Thus, although it is in fact well known to most serious students of politics, it is not exactly a popular term. Further, it is very little known outside of the United States. Practically no Englishman who has not made a special study of public choice is aware of what the term means.

Log-rolling in its simplest form is simply a trade among voters as to what they will vote for in which they agree to vote against something which they actually favor when their feeling is feeble in return for somebody else assisting them getting something they want. Suppose, for example, that there are two bills before the legislative body. One legislator is strongly in favor of bill *A*, but on the whole opposed to bill *B*. Another legislator is strongly in favor of bill *B*, but only mildly opposed to bill *A*. If they agree to both vote to pass bills *A* and *B* they in each case give up their preferences on some place where they are mild in order to get their preferences where they are strong and this is a mutually advantageous agreement. This bargain could be done either by exchange of promises, for example the first voter agrees to vote for

B tomorrow if the second voter will vote for *A* today, or by creating a new combined bill *AB*.

There are many clear-cut examples of this. It used to be true in boss-dominated American cities, for example, that each linguistic minority would have the machine nominate an appropriate number of their members for each job. As an example which has been mentioned many times in the press, in New York the school system was Jewish, the police Irish, and the sanitation work Italian. This of course was some time ago, now Puerto Ricans and blacks have to be recognized too.

It should be noted that there are not all that many of these log-rolling groups when one turns to the voters voting on actual provisions. The reason for this is simple, and that is the vote is secret and hence it is possible for anyone who wishes to promise to vote for all the machine candidates and actually only vote for one or two and cast the rest of his votes in accordance with his preference. When we deal with open voting, however, this kind of thing is dominant. College faculties do a great deal of this kind of thing.

This example is obviously simple, but a good deal of it goes on. When we turn to actual legislatures the matters are much more complicated and the word log-rolling is sometimes reserved for these very complicated businesses. A single bill will be designed to provide benefits to the constituents of a whole collection of different congressmen. Later a congressman will vote for one bill under the guarantee that some months in the future something else to their benefit will come through. Further, frequently the trade is not well specified. 'You help me here and I will help you later sometime.' This is the way that all legislatures work.

To repeat a story which I have told before, a very intelligent MP, who eventually became a cabinet minister, had dinner with me. I asked him whether this business of trading votes occurred in the British House of Commons and he indignantly denied that it did. 'Nothing like that occurred,' he said. The following day he gave a public speech. The speech dealt with his activities as a member of the House of Commons and he said: 'You go to committees which you are totally uninterested in and vote as somebody wants and then you take him to your committee and hold up his hand.'

He was an intelligent man and quite reasonable when I pointed out the contradiction. He immediately recognized it himself and in fact looked a little embarrassed. I think that a great many politicians who are accustomed to doing just exactly this are not accustomed to talking about it or having other people talk about it and hence are apt to deny it. Further, political bodies, student governments in particular, are rather apt to pass laws saying it is illegal to log-roll. This does not prevent them from doing it and in fact these laws are frequently passed with the aid of such vote trades.

With this definition problem out of the way let us turn to the use of the concept. The first chapters in this book were devoted to a very simple model and in general reached only elementary conclusions. We now move to a more realistic situation. In this chapter we will, however, retain a model where the citizens vote directly on the issues rather than having representatives. We go on to more realistic situations where representatives vote on specific issues later.

Switzerland in recent years has been switching more and more towards direct voting on issues and in fact students are beginning to say it is not a representative republic but a direct democracy. Some of the Cantons always had a similar rule. Zurich is an example. The Council passed various laws but the law was then, unless it was urgent, put on hold until the next general public election, and then all the laws passed by the legislature were submitted to the public.

The public usually simply ratified them. This is not surprising granted that a number of them were such things as repairing a given street, or hiring three additional policeman. There were cases in which the popular vote might have an effect. For many years popular votes prevented the Zurich cantonal council from building a subway and more recently popular votes forced the city council to retain a loss making art theater.

Considering direct votes, we automatically think of California, but most western states have a good many things put up to direct vote. The reader may recall a situation in which Oregon presented the voters with a long list of diseases and they were to check ones for which the government was to provide medical treatment. It turned out that the voters were reasonably discriminating although not perfectly so. They did not want to spend an infinite amount of money trying to cure all diseases.

There are of course town meetings still in many places in New England. Since considerable time investment is necessary to attend town meetings it is not obvious that you get either close to the total population or a random sample of it.

To begin our analysis, there are a few technical points. Firstly almost all direct votes are up-down votes on some proposition. In other words, it is the yes/no kind of thing in which majority voting is most likely to be a correct method. But I say most likely, not is highly likely. Minorities with intense feelings can be and frequently are injured.

This may be a good point to begin the discussion of what I believe is the actual basic voting used in most democracies. Many dictatorships, monarchies, etc., also use a decision method which resembles it. Let us suppose the following system which as I start will not seem very much like what we observe in the real-world, but I will later complicate it so that it does. Suppose then that anybody who wishes may make a proposal to be put up to popular vote. In the mail yesterday I received a solicitation for funds by a citizens' organization that wishes to start the process for amending the constitution. What they want is to introduce an amendment which would mean that the present trust fund in the Social Security System would be abolished.

The reader may recall that some time ago Senator Monohan, a highly skilled and intelligent politician, also made an effort to get this done although the details were different. He failed completely and I presume that these people also will fail. In any event, I am not sending them any money.

I should perhaps say that my reason for not sending them any money is not that I think their proposal undesirable. Indeed, I regard the Federal Social Security Trust Fund as a fraud and a scandal. It resembles a great deal the arrangement that Robert Maxwell had for the pensions of his employees and in his case when it began to show signs of being exposed he committed suicide by jumping off his private yacht. The yacht apparently had been largely paid for out of the fraud.

To return to this model suppose then that anyone who wishes may make up a proposal and these proposals are put in a hopper, from time to time one is drawn out and voted on. I should say that the state of Arizona in the upcoming election will have ten referendum proposals on the ballot and of these ten some have been presented by the legislature or other government bodies, but a good many are private initiatives.

Let us temporarily ignore how such proposals are made up. We earlier talked about the fact that we do not have very much data, and just go on with the process. One is drawn out of the hat and is then debated by a various people, newspapers, etc., and eventually voted on. The vote is either yes or no. If it is yes it is enacted into law and we are all expected to respect it. If it is no it is discarded, but the people who put it up are free to present it or a modified version of it for future referendum by putting it in the hopper where it will be eligible again to be drawn at random. Granted that a lot of people will put them in, the delay for another bill to be brought up is likely to be high.

Note that this avoids the Arrow problem partly because of the likely long delay and the uncertainty of when the matter will actually come up, and partly because you only have a yes/no vote.

Note that this model that I have got can be modified to be very close to the way in which legislatures vote, and for that matter, the way that kings, whether they are geniuses, like Henry VII, or dolts, like Louis XVI, make decisions. Various things are presented to them, they say yes or no and that is that; however, the courtiers are free to start the process again getting other things in.

The second technical problem is that they do not always use majority voting. It used to be indeed that most states required considerably more than a majority, and normally of property owners only, to pass any bond issue. There are still some remnants of this around, but in general they have been knocked out.

In passing, although this is not directly relevant to this chapter, a somewhat similar knocking out of an above majority requirement was carried out by the Supreme Court in one of its more bizarre decisions. It decided that the Constitution of the United States, which of course, provides for a Senate and a House, with the Senate elected in a very, very disproportionate way, prohibited states from having the same kind of a system. Trees, the Supreme Court said, do not vote unless of course it is in Alaska and they are voting for the U.S. Senate.

The result of this is that they do not need as many voters in favor of an issue to push the two houses of the legislature to pass a bill as you would if the two houses were elected differently. State expenditures as a share of the total income of the states have increased since this Supreme Court decision was made, although whether that is the cause is not obvious.

Returning to direct popular votes, the two-thirds or higher majority for bond issues which might increase the total cost of government was very traditional in the United States. It is hard to argue that something which was characteristic of most parts of the United States for a very long time was 'undemocratic.'

When people are presented with a simple yes/no choice, which is true of all of these direct votes except the city town meetings in

New England, where does the issue that they are being asked to vote on come from?

In many places you simply need a petition signed by a certain number of people to put such a proposition on the ballot. In large states the number needed is very large, and even in Switzerland, where this method is widely used, the cost of the petition is significant enough to make it a real hazard for many propositions which otherwise would no doubt be voted for by the voters.

Note that this means that for propositions which are of any degree of complexity, and as a matter of fact most of them are, the decisions of what collection of specific provisions will be put in the thing to be voted on by the people is not made by the people themselves, but by some person or group which is trying to put together a bill which will attract a majority of the voters.

Sometimes these proposals put up to the voters are put together by some governmental body, the city council for example, and sometimes by private citizens. Taking the second first, I have never been involved in preparing a petition and soliciting signatures, etc. (there are professional petition signer/gatherers), although I have friends who have. It is not an easy process.

First, it should be pointed out that in general the stronger you make the proposal, the less likely it will pass. On the other hand, the weaker you make it, the less interested you are in whether it passes or not. This normally leads to a lot of discussion while these things are being drawn up with some people wanting to make the language stronger and broader, and others wanting to narrow it. We do not, in general, have any record of this kind of discussion. It is usually informal with no records kept. Further, people can join or leave the groups making up the referendum proposal more or less at will. Sometimes there are several groups trying to draft proposals on somewhat the same subject.

Once the thing has been drawn up and a suitable number of signatures collected (not infrequently the proposal is drawn up and does not get enough signatures) then there is a vote and it either passes or does not. If it fails, there may be further efforts with slightly different language in the petition. Even if it succeeds, there is always the possibility that somebody else will try and get a reversal through the referendum process. Some of the western states actually have provisions for a repeal in their constitutions.

After the event there is usually a good deal of congratulations by the people who put it up if they won, and incrimination if they lost. To repeat, I have never been in on the actual discussion, but apparently it is long and protracted and there is no formal procedure, so there can be all sorts of differences of opinion, which are not ended by a simple majority vote.

I should say that a certain amount of empirical work has been done about such things as the egg control board in Vancouver, etc. As a rule of thumb, it is harder for special interests to get special cartel procedures through referendum than it is to get them through the legislature. Why it is easier to get them through the legislature will be discussed later, but the fact that they are harder apparently to get through a referendum does appear to be clear.

Having said this which is obviously an advantage of the referendum over the legislative route, it should be pointed out that the people who vote on the referendum are usually much less well informed about what the bill actually provides, etc., than are the legislators.

To repeat an extreme case, and there is no actual referendum in this case, but one can see what would happen, *The New York Times* carried a long table of statistics of various sorts on the minimum wage. Taking two of these statistics[2] 84 percent of the American citizens think that the minimum wage law should be raised and 78 percent of them do not know what the legal minimum wage now is. It is clear that at the very least 62 percent of the citizens who do not know what the minimum wage is think that it should be increased.

Congressmen are frequently confused and ignorant, but not that ignorant. It is also true that in general congressmen know more about what their constituents think about a given bill than about the bill itself. This is to be expected granted the fact that they depend on their constituents to be reelected.

For myself, I have always liked the situation that was described above in Zurich. The city council passes bills taking advantage of their presumably superior knowledge, then it is submitted to popular vote, with the result that special interest legislation is less likely to get through than it would had it just been done by the city council.

With this procedure, even if the citizens had normally ratified whatever the city council wants it does not mean they have not had influence. The city council, knowing that they will eventually vote, proceed to give popular opinion considerable weight in their decisions. Measures that they think will not get through the popular vote are never presented to the populace at all.

There was for a while an interesting case of this sort in Florida in which instead of presenting the citizens with an appropriation or bond issue proposal with a simple up/down vote on something that the board of education had decided on, they were given the right to write in what they thought was the right amount. The vote then would be counted in such a way that the median preference won.

This was eventually abolished because the citizens rarely took advantage of this privilege. This could indicate that they did not care, or it could also indicate that the legislature, in this case the school board, realized that they could not get away with anything and hence did not try.

This naturally brings us the situation where some government body draws up the proposal which is put to the populace. In the United States, more often than not, this kind of thing comes in connection with bond issues or other kinds of expenditure. The voters, of course, do not have any right to amend the proposal. Although they have no right to amend the proposal they can have some influence in changing it.

To recur to my favorite example, almost immediately after I moved to Tucson, the city government put up a bond issue for a whole collection of different things including street repairs, school improvements, etc.. It was voted down. The city council responded to this by saying that the basic problem was that they had not put in enough projects in for people living in the southeastern part of town. They added such projects and held a number of local meetings to see if people in each district were specifically interested in the issue, put it up again and it passed. Of course, it is not true that the outcome satisfied everyone.

The fact that not everyone is satisfied is a pretty much necessary requirement when you have activities that are carried on which of necessity require quite a lot of people to be covered. Some almost certainly will dislike it. The point of voting is to in so far as possible select a system in which the costs inflicted on people who are unhappy are less than the benefits gained by those who are happy. Unfortunately as we will see it is not possible that this is always true, but we can at least in some sense approximate it.

It should be emphasized here that somewhat the same kind of problem occurs in the market. It is true that if I go into a drug store looking for something for athlete's foot I will see a dozen or so different remedies on display and can choose the one I want.[3]

This is not total freedom. Suppose I knew a good deal about these medicines and I would prefer something that was different from any of them. If I were the only person or there were only a few persons that had those preferences it would never be offered in the market. The economy of scale in producing large numbers of almost any product are such that the designers attempt, just like the designers of a political bill, to attract as many people as they can, but do not expect that everyone will like it.

The difference in the market over the government here is that it is likely because of the choice and the variety that fewer people are disappointed in the market than with the government action. This is not because the government method of making decisions is inherently inferior, but because of the fact that the type of goods that the government should deal with are ones where a certain number of people have to be denied their choices.

For many things it is a necessity for even modest efficiency that all the people in a sizeable geographical area consume the same product. Thus, individual choice on a product by product basis is impossible and necessarily people will be disappointed, but this is not an example of democracy being inferior to the market, it is a statement that certain goods we wish to consume cannot be handled on a completely individual choice basis.

Agenda control will be briefly discussed here. In fact, my previous example of bond issue in Tucson was a rather deviant example of it. There is a standard case that occurs in referendums which can be dealt with here.

This was first discovered dealing with Oregon school appropriation issues. Suppose that last year a school of some particular district expended $100,000,000 and the school bureaucracy wants to spend as much as possible this year. The maximum proposal that they can make with a good chance on passing depends on what is called the reversion level, what happens if it fails.

For example, if they put up an amount of money and it is voted down they automatically get last year's appropriation. Under these circumstances they better not ask for too large of an increase. Suppose on the other hand the legislature has provided that if there is a vote on the school budget by the citizens and it fails the budget is automatically 10 percent less than last year.

It is clear these two situations are different. In one case it is a choice between $100,000,000 and whatever the school board suggests and the other $90,000,000 and whatever the school board suggests. The school board can safely offer a higher amount in the second case and the empirical evidence indicates that they know this and do it.

As a somewhat similar phenomenon, the line item veto has had very little effect in the states in which it is available. The reason for this is that if the governor vetoes a particular line that means that he is giving the legislature a choice between that particular amount and zero. Mostly the legislature does not prefer zero and the governor, knowing this, does not veto a line. There is another procedure called recision, in which the governor is not required to veto, but can just make a reduction. The number of states that have this is not large enough for firm statistical tests, but it would appear that in this case it does indeed lower the total expenditure. The governor can give the legislature the choice between the amount they voted for and 95 percent of that amount and he normally prevails.

So far in this chapter we have overlooked an important problem, which is exactly what is necessary to get in the way of a vote to pass something through a popular referendum. We may require a majority, more than a majority, say two-thirds, which is not uncommon for constitutional matters, perhaps less than a majority, say 40 percent. I find that many people take the view that the latter is an unacceptable requirement, although during the term of President Clinton, one would think that it would not be as common as an objection as it had been before. As a matter of fact, as I mentioned before Lincoln, Wilson and Kennedy were all elected without a majority of the popular vote.

I am not particularly in favor of less than the majority votes, but I think that I should give it a little attention here partly because I got personally involved.

In the *Calculus of Consent* we set off the legislative costs, the difficulty of putting together a suitable large coalition against the actual cost of the issue and chose the case where the total cost was minimized. Unfortunately, I put in a couple of lines in which I said for very unimportant matters less than a majority would probably be the appropriate number. This has been objected to more than any other single thing in that book. Dennis Mueller, past president of the Public Choice Society, friend of mine and an authority in the area, has written a set of rather general surveys of the literature. *Public Choice II*[4] has a diagram which is intended to show that less than the majority is impossible.

The objection made again and again by all of the objectors is that if you have less than a majority requirement, then one candidate elected by say 43 percent may be replaced by someone else with 43 percent. There may be two inconsistent proposals each of which could get more than 40 percent of the vote. One bill being passed it might be reversed the following day. You will remember from Chapter 4 that this is also possible with majority rule as it is normally practiced, but for the time being, let us consider the issue as presented by the objectors. I should repeat here that I have only devoted a couple sentences to what I thought was a very unimportant matter in *The Calculus of Consent*.

To repeat, it is fairly common for people to have less than a majority vote, our current president did. The way this is done is simple and straight forward. A number of candidates or proposals are put up, the one that gets the most votes, 43 percent in the case of President Clinton is declared elected and the repeat election in which a loser tries again is not permitted. Whether it is a good system or not I leave open because in a later chapter when we are discussing the election of officials rather than direct voting we will devote considerable time to that issue.

In order to insure that we have a majority, it is essential that we confine the election to a choice between two alternatives. This can be done either by putting up only two alternatives, let us say, parking in certain areas shall or shall not be illegal, or by letting a number of alternatives be put up, for example, people running in a primary election, and then providing for a run off between the top two.

Both of these have fairly severe defects which will be dealt with later but we should point out here that either one of them may eliminate an alternative which could beat either of the two in the final round. It is necessary here as in the case where we permit 40 percent or some lower percentage to prohibit additional votes in order to make sure that you have a decisive outcome.

When the republicans successfully nominated Goldwater in 1964 and the democrats McGovern in 1980, the populace was presented with a choice between two people and one of them got a majority. In both cases if the republicans on the one hand and the democrats on the other had chosen a more centrist figure they might well have beaten the man who actually won the election. If there had been three candidates, another compromise candidate in addition to these three its quite possible that one of the three would have gotten a majority, as Lincoln did not in 1860.

There is another major problem, a problem in all methods of voting. Who is to vote? Here I am not going to raise questions which will be discussed later whether we should be somewhat selective about voters, but the fact is that in general not everybody votes at all. Town meetings in New England may have less than 10 percent of the registered voters present. Any other votes either on issues like the bond issue which I mentioned earlier or on the direct election of citizens have quite a large number of people voting. Australia, and some cantons in Switzerland, have dealt with this problem by fining people that do not vote.

If we are concerned about less than the majority voting because it could lead to a reversal later, we should be concerned with less number of people actually voting than the total electorate. This could again permit reversals later.

Most legislative bodies, sometimes this applies to direct popular vote, have quorum requirements. A certain number of people have to be present in voting in order for a bill to be passed or rejected. Quorum requirements are normally about half of the legislature.

The reason they are low is if they are set at two-thirds, then 40 percent of the legislature can prevent any given bill from passing. A two-thirds quorum vote would be equivalent to a two-thirds majority requirement. This might be wise, but it should not be done as a by-product of the quorum rule.

It is interesting that some people claim that the American constitution was never properly ratified because in some of the state conventions the necessary quorum was above a majority. This would permit a large minority to prevent ratification by simply staying away. The state conventions did what at that time was customary. They sent out the sheriffs and arrested the missing members of the legislature. They were brought in tied to their chairs and thus this made up the quorum to vote. This was an experiment we do not want repeated.

If you worry about the prospect that a bill once being passed by a less than majority vote could be reversed by another less than majority vote, you should consider the prospect that it may be reversed if people who did not vote that first time do so again. The reasons people do not vote in elections are many and various, and its not at all obvious that those who do vote are a representative random collection. I would say it is obvious they are not.

It is probable that people do not vote because to some extent they are not interested in the subject. Furthermore, public opinion polling normally does not turn up a strong evidence that the election would be reversed if the non-voters voted. This latter item is less significant than you might think because of the strong tendency of people who did not vote to report that they would have voted with the way that the majority went. There is even a tendency for people who voted with the minority to later report to pollsters that they voted with the majority. Thus less than a majority vote is by no means impossible. I recommended that it should be used for unimportant matters. I do not regard the election of the President of the United States as an unimportant matter.

We return to the other possibility of not having simple majority voting, but requiring more than a majority. We can begin at the bottom. In Switzerland, amending the constitution can be done by direct popular vote which must have a majority for the amendment in the country as a whole, and also an independent majority in each of a majority of the cantons. Obviously, this is a somewhat higher requirement than a simple majority in the nation as a whole, and occasionally a proposed amendment fails because of this. It is only slightly higher than a simple majority. It is equivalent to let us say 52 percent as a majority requirement.

Another example, which we mentioned in *The Calculus of Consent* concerns zoning variances. The rough rule of thumb in general used is that such variances will be turned down if more than 20 percent of the people in the immediate vicinity object to it. This is an 80 percent majority rule, and I should perhaps emphasize that this area differs from place to place, and the area which people can exercise this veto power is not clearly delineated in most cases. Tucson is 320 feet.[5]

There are in the United States some 30,000 homeowners association or condominium developments. These are uniformly started by a real estate developer who purchases land, and incorporates the homeowners association as the governing body of the land for many purposes.[6] They proceed to build houses or big apartment buildings, and the houses or apartments are then sold to individuals who have a vote in the homeowners association.

The real estate people who build these things no doubt design the charter which they give to the purchasers (it is a sort of constitution for that development), in order to attract purchasers. They design it in what they think is the most attractive from the standpoint of future citizens of their little community. It is interesting that they almost always have in it somewhere provisions that at least some changes in the charter can only be made by direct vote, usually more than a majority.

This is a fair indication that people do prefer to have some things put to more than a majority vote. The American constitution is another example, but since we inherit that rather than making free choices it is less convincing.

It should be said that these homeowners association frequently have weighted voting with the people who own the more expensive accommodations having more votes than those who have cheap accommodations. It is also true that in general the voting is by residence, not by head. In other words, in the one that I live in at the moment I have as many votes as the married couple next door. Once again everybody has entered into these agreements voluntarily, and the people who draw them up, the real estate firms, have every motive to choose what they think is the most attractive form of charter, so we can assume that this is well accepted by present day people.

This will serve as an introduction to a more general question of 'who should vote?' Most of my readers will think immediately and automatically that all adults except criminals and lunatics should be permitted to vote. It should be said that at one point the supreme court looked as through it was going to declare that all lunatics and criminals could vote.

To repeat, this raises a number of questions, the first is 'who is an adult?' Immediately after World War II a tribe in Northern New Guinea who had been impressed by visiting Americans organized a democratic constitution in which an adult was defined as any one over the age 10. In prewar Japan, to vote you had to be 25 and a male to vote. In general, this is the range I have been able to find in reasonably modern institutions, but it should be said that F.A. Hayek in his proposals for constitutional reform has one house of the legislature elected by voters who are middle-aged or elderly. In the rather vigorous discussion that his proposals have aroused this particular aspect has seldom been criticized.

Actually, the question of how old you have to be to vote is pretty much an open one. Recently we lowered the voting age to 18 for males.[7] Congress shortly after it had approved an amendment to the constitution lowering the voting age to 18 for males decided that people between the ages 18 and 21 could not buy alcoholic beverages. They could vote but not drink.

Mathematically, the subject is an interesting one because it does not appear to make very much difference. When you raise the voting age you increase the weight of the individual voter when he finally does reach that age. Let us temporarily assume that there is a discount rate of zero on political power. Let us contrast the New Guinea tribe mentioned above with the 10 year old adult rule and with Japan where it was 25.

The 10 year rule would permit the person to vote from the time he was 10 on, but his vote would be diluted by the fact that many other people were voting. In other words, the Japanese voting after age of 25 would vote in fewer elections, but his vote would count more simply because there were fewer people voting.

Retaining our zero discount rate, the situation is interesting because changes in the majority rule when you can begin to vote, have a peculiar effect. Suppose that the voting age is lowered from 21 to 18, as it was for men in the United States. With zero discount new voters over their life span have about the same situation[8]

Lowering the voting age does not benefit the people who are under the new voting age as their lifetime political power would be the same. It unambiguously injures those people who are over the new minimum at the time of change, because their power for the rest of their life has been reduced. The people within the bracket 21 to 18 will lose but not much because the vote will be diluted, but on the other hand they get some additional time to cast it even if not enough for full compensation.

If you raise the voting age interestingly it does not injure the people who are under the old voting age limit. They have fewer votes, but each vote counts for more. Those over the new age limit unambiguously gain.

All of this is changed if one assumes that there is a discount rate for political power that is greater than zero. Since the young people have a low voting rate, it would appear on the whole they do not have a high discount rate on political power. None of this indicates what voting age we should have in this area. Most discussion of the matter ignores the effect of increasing the number of people who can vote on the power of the individual voter, but perhaps the discount rate is high, and it should be ignored.

There are other possible restrictions. In the first place only citizens are permitted to vote in most places, although it is not at all obvious why this should be true. They are affected by the outcome of the vote. Still, more or less, this is a pretty uniform rule. The United States is moving to voting methods which will probably permit a lot of aliens to vote, although the votes will be illegally cast. In general, the recent voting reforms have made the old-fashioned boss dominated corrupt votes much easier than they were since the reforms of the late 19th and early 20th century which were inspired by a desire to eliminate that kind of corrupt voting.

There are other prospects. During most of history of the United States, in many states you had to be able to read and write in order to vote. This was abolished because southern states had been using it as a way to discriminate against blacks.

If we assume that it is not used as a way to discriminate against blacks, it has much to be said for it. The requirement that one must be able to read and write in order to vote seems to be a minimal requirement for information.

I bring the subject up because Dennis Mueller, a prominent Public Choice scholar has discussed it very favorably in his *Constitutional Democracy*.[9] He also suggested that it might be desirable to give an examination to everybody who wants to vote. He would suggest an examination which could be designed not to discriminate against people on racial or economic grounds but to discriminate in terms, more or less, of whether they have remembered what was taught in high school civics.

This is not our present law, but assuming that there is no discrimination it is a little hard to argue that people who do not know what is going on in the government should be permitted to control it. On the other hand, if we were more extreme, and insisted on them being really well-informed, it is likely we would only get 5 or 6 percent of the population voting. Whether this would be a good or bad thing, I do not know. I am simply discussing it here because it has been suggested.

Another way of restricting the vote, which has been seriously suggested is that a sizeable random sample about 1,000 eligible voters be selected about a year before an upcoming election and they be the only people permitted to vote in this election. They would individually have vastly more power than do under ordinary circumstances, they would have strong incentives to become well informed. Further, the various political machines could concentrate their information activities on this little group of 1,000 or so voters.

You would have to take precautions to make certain that these 1,000 people did not, one way or the other, sell their vote. Special acts of congress after the election in which all of the people in this group were given a trip to the Caribbean (shall we say) as a reward for their work would have to be made strictly unconstitutional. It would be particularly so if only one of the parties was offering it.

This collection of restrictions on voting has been offered because, in general, they are not discussed at all. In general, the increase in the franchise is simply regarded as obviously good as long as it is confined to national citizens. The steady steps in the 19th century by which the franchise was extended to more parts of the English population are normally praised.[10]

Extensions of the franchise are normally voted by an existing government which for one reason or another thinks it will help them in the next election. In a way, politically it is rather like the habit in both France and Greece of changing the election rules before most elections in order to keep the present government in power. In all three of these cases extension of the franchise, and the changing of the election rules in France and Greece, it turns out that the people who do it are not very good at understanding the actual dynamics election and they frequently lose.

This discussion of who should vote so far has dealt with matters where we do not have any clear idea of whether it is good or bad. There is another major change that was made by most countries in recent years which can be argued is highly desirable. This was permitting women to vote. The effect of this has been sizeable changes in the legal status of women. Considering temporarily only the Anglo-Saxon countries, the common law which was used up to the change gave women quite a number of legal disabilities as contrasted to men. Once women could vote these were quickly eliminated and this was clearly a step in the right direction. It is very hard to argue that women voting have been any particular improvement on other matters. They are very large (50 percent) random sample of the population on most, but not all, issues.

It is usually true that at least some things dealt with by public opinion polls that the women are different from the men, but it is very hard to argue that they are better or worse in their judgment than the men.[11] Thus, if we ignore the status problems it is very hard to say whether it was a good idea or bad, but since the women, in general, want the vote and there is no point in picking quarrels with them, I certainly will not recommend that they be deprived of it.

In a way this issue is rather like a proposal that people whose names are in the last half of the alphabet will not be permitted to vote. This would be a large random sample, and I presume if we took public opinion polls on this standard we would find that there were differences but there would be no reason to believe that one side was better than the other.

The decision mentioned above to reduce the number of voters to a random sample of 1,000 would have the effect that the information of those 1,000 would be much better by the time the election came about than that of the ordinary voter. This is hardly an expected effect when you take these very large random samples, like women or the second half of the alphabet.

Finally, there is one proposal for reducing the voting population which I am in favor of and have mentioned several times in my writings, and that is the people who are dependent upon the government for their livelihood should not be permitted to vote because they will have the strongest possible motive to vote almost entirely in terms of their own personal income.

---

[1] University of Michigan Press, Ann Arbor (1962).

[2] *New York Times*, April 19, 1996 A1.

[3] This may not be all that helpful. Recently I had a bad case of athlete's foot, and put a standard remedy on it for quite some time. It seemed to get worse, I finally went to a doctor and he informed me that I was allergic to an ingredient contained in all non-prescription athletes foot cures.

[4] Cambridge, 1989 he devotes pages 55 and 56 largely to this issue. He has since produced another book *Constitutional Democracy*. (Oxford, 1996) in which he favors reinforced majorities for many issues, but his figures on pages 154-5 repeat his earlier demonstration.

[5] A recent developer purchased a large plot of land that he wanted to use for development which required a zoning variance, but applied for the zoning variance only for that part of the land that was more than 320 feet from its boundary. It avoided the 80 percent rule, although he had other difficulties.

[6] They are not legally a local government, but they function much like it.

[7] It had always been 18 for females after they were permitted to vote.

[8] It should be noted that if the minimum voting age was raised to 75 this would remain true. Your expectancy of political power would be the same. Once again this depends on our zero discount rate. This assumes that you are willing to take

the chance of a very strong and powerful vote if you live to 75, rather than a lifetime of much weaker votes.

[9] Oxford 1996.

[10] It only ended in 1930 when the franchise was extended to the last remaining women.

[11] At the moment women are more likely to vote Democratic than men. Amusingly the press normally reports this as a 'gender gap' problem for the Republicans, although it is as easy to argue that the Democrats have the opposite gender gap.

CHAPTER 7
More Complicated Log-Rolling

So far in talking about votes and log-rolling, we have used very simple bargains. As a matter of fact as you will note if you go back to look at the examples in Chapter 3, the real legislative bargains are frequently complicated. It is sensible to discuss these complicated types of log-rolling bargains before we turn to the question of election of legislators themselves. Although the intention of this chapter is to deal with complicated log-rolling bargains, I am going to try to use reasonably simple models, not the models we have used before, but still not too complicated.

In general log-rolling can take either one of two forms. There is what I call explicit log-rolling in which I agree to vote for something that you want in return for you agreeing at some later date to vote for something I want. The other type is implicit log-rolling where we stick the two items into the same bill.

Mathematically and theoretically I see little difference, but a number of people have seen a very great moral difference. Duncan Black, for example, thought that the first type was viciously immoral, but the second type was all right. His argument was that in the first type the person agreed to vote for something that he did not actually approve of, hence his vote was lying. In the second type, although he would naturally have preferred not to have to vote for part of the act, he favored the whole bill, and hence was not lying.

I feel that this was a little naive since the bill had to be put together somehow, and putting it together would involve the same kind of 'lying' as actually voting against your preferences in the legislature, rather than in the committee. Although there are people who regard this as important, I do not, and the distinction will be slid over in my examples.

As is customary in dealing with these things I will start with a very simple model. We will, for a start, assume that there are only three legislators. These legislators would, in fact, be motivated by a desire to win the next election and hence represent individual citizens. Later we will discuss in a general way more than three.

The use of three is for reasons of simplicity, but as a matter of fact, very small groups of the sort that I am talking about here, if we turn to the real world, would begin to show signs of small group social interaction, and the type of bargaining that I am talking about would be replaced by something more complicated. I am going to ignore these small group effects and assume that the meeting is impersonal even if the number of people meeting each other is small enough so that does not seem very reasonable.

Let us now consider a three person legislature as shown in Table 7.1 where Mr. 1, Mr. 2, and Mr. 3, are choosing among three alternatives, A, B, and C. In each case, a majority vote of no on each alternative means the status quo remains in that particular field. As a concrete example, assume that each of them is a proposal to build a school in a different part of the city. Note that these numbers are not just the tax or expenditure, but the strength of the preferences or aversions of these people.

As you can see, in this case these numbers make bargaining possible. Various coalitions are possible as shown in Table 7.2.

Indeed, if all three of them were passed, in other words, a unanimity requirement, the outcome would be Pareto optimal, but Mr. 3 would neither gain nor lose, the other two would gain.

Table 7.1: Strength of preferences

Alternatives	1	2	3
A	7	-1	-2
B	-1	5	-4
C	-4	0	6

Table 7.2: Payoff to coalitions

		1	2	3
1,2	(A,B)	6	4	-6
2,3	(B,C)	-5	5	2
1,3	(C,A)	3	-1	4
1,2,3	(A,B,C)	2	4	0

But any pair can do better in a two-man coalition. In each of these coalitions, as can be seen from Table 7.2, the third man, the one who is left out, not only gains nothing but actually loses. This illustrates the occurrence of external costs in governmental actions. The reader may notice that there is a cycle among these three coalitions. In this case the cycle is accidental, but with larger numbers of voters and alternatives, it is almost inevitable.

Note that the existence of the cycle does not necessarily lead to any difficulties. In the procedure normally used to put matters up for a vote any of the coalitions could carry their proposals. This is true whether the matters are put up as a group of two or possibly three for a single vote or whether there are successive votes with the trade being honored. Assuming the members kept their bargains there would be no cycle. This, although the numbers in this table are accidental, is an illustration of the point that standard methods of voting in which things are put up for yes/no votes and if they lose put back in que for vote again at do not produce cycles even if the raw preferences are cyclicalsome.

Note, however, that if there were other things which would be exchanged, or you could simply make cash payments, another bargain could be made. A bargain between any two of these could not be replaced by a bargain by another pair, because that would damage the credit of persons who entered into the first bargain and then switched. If you are to continue playing you cannot ruin your credit.

In the real world straight cash payments are generally barred, but there are very large number of other bills, clauses, and so forth. Also payoff by one of them is always available. Presumably, these different clauses are worth different amounts. As we have discussed before, there is some particular bargain which has a higher total value than any of the others. In other words, it is rather like a market situation in which one assumes that victory will go to the highest bidding group.

Nevertheless, granted the secrecy which people maintain for their own preferences, it is possible that we would never find that particular combination which had the highest group payoff. It is also possible that we would, but we can say that the bargain would always improve the outcome unless there were serious mistakes.

In any event, the bargaining is likely to end with something being put up to vote, and being either accepted or turned down. If it is accepted, it is unlikely under most rules of procedure that contrary bargains would be permitted on the floor in that particular session of a legislative body.

In a way the cycle is stopped by two things, one of which is the bargaining process, and the second is the fact that many votes on the issue are temporarily restricted. In practice as we have pointed out before it is likely that everybody will get something at either one or the other of these bargains, and there is no strong pressure to repeal any single one of them.

Looking at our simple little group it is fairly obvious that two has less to gain from coalitions as opposed to the Pareto optimum that the others, but that does not mean that he will not gain. Voters 1 and 3 have very strong motives for entering into some coalition, but unfortunately their preferences are almost diametrically opposed. The coalitions as I have drawn them up are not by any means the only possible coalitions if other matters are to be voted on.

In this example the problem does not arise, but in many cases somebody might be motivated to vote in favor of something that will actually injure him in order to avoid greater injury. We can design another matrix with that characteristic, but since it is obvious I do not think that it is worth while.

In this case the only way of getting a majority is getting a two-thirds majority. Still, unanimity would be arguably desirable. If we just drew lots and let each one of them, one after another, choose an alternative, interestingly enough they would end up with the Pareto solution also. I would not like to argue that this is a general phenomenon, it happens to be true in this particular matrix.

Logically, we should now go on to a larger matrix of voters. Unfortunately, this becomes too complicated to handle on the pages of a book. For example, if there are five voters choosing among five alternatives there are ten possible coalitions with a simple majority vote, and five if there is an 80 percent majority required. Adding in a unanimity requirement means that there would be sixteen horizontal lines in our tables. Having had a great deal of difficulty avoiding arithmetic errors on the three by three table, I would suspect that some would creep in on this larger one. If we move to realistic numbers, even if not 435, the problem would become completely unmanageable. We might compete with Archimedes' sand reckoner.

If we assume as we did in a prior chapter that there is a good deal of symmetry in the problem, specifically that each of them wants a particular expenditure and does not like paying taxes for any of the others clearly we will get the kind of situation described in the road model. Reading Stockman's discussion of the Federal soup kitchen, you get the impression that this is what is going on there, but it is not true that all of the projects were worth the same amounts, or that the tax cost falling on other people was always the same. Thus, this would be much more complex.

To repeat, we are dealing here with professional legislators who have lots of time and money, and professional assistants. They are organized in committees, small coalitions, and parties. All of these can act as intermediaries within the legislature. Of course, the fact that in the American legislature there are two houses, and the bargain that will get you through one does not necessarily get you through the other, makes it more complex.

The general structure of what goes on is fairly obvious. An individual or small group thinks of putting forward some issue. It might be a formal committee or a subcommittee of Congress, a group of people with similar views who have in the past voted together, or one of the parties.[1] It is much like the situation I was talking about earlier in which a few citizens decided they would like to have a Green Belt along the Iowa River.

They are trying to maximize their own preferences, but they know they must get it through the legislature, or the popular vote, as the case may be. Thus, they try to get the most that they can for themselves, but remember, they are a coalition with different interests to some extent, while still making it something that has a good chance of getting through the whole legislature.

When you have a two-house legislature, like the United States, you have the problem of getting it through two houses, and the personnel in the two houses, elected by different ways, may have different preferences. In the individual states, since the Supreme Court decided that the Federal Constitution required that the two houses in a state both be elected on a per capita basis, these problems are easier because what gets a winning coalition in one house is apt to have it in the other.

There are sometimes cases in which the two houses disagree on details but agree on the main point. The standard rule is if there are differences between the two houses in a bill which is generally similar, it is referred to a conference committee drawn from both houses. The result of this conference committee is a report which 'merges' the two and is put to a vote with no amendments permitted.

There was a period of time in which people in both houses of Congress were attempting to get restrictions on appropriations for the Institute for Humanities prohibiting it from funding pornographic material. When put to vote in the form of an amendment, it won overwhelmingly in both houses. The con-ference committee always deleted it. The apparent reason was that a majority in at least one house did not like the provision, but wanted to conceal their dislike from the voters.

There are a number of things that come out of this simple straightforward model, which are also characteristic of the more complicated world. Let us now turn to discussing these.

The 'A,B' coalition has the highest point payoff for its members and is higher than the total Pareto payoff. On the other hand, taking all three into account, the 'A,B,C' coalition has the same total payoff as the 'A,B' coalition. 'A' loses, 'B' stays the same, and 'C' gains, but the losses and gains more or less cancel.

This particular log-rolling game differs from the earlier one on roads. The coalition of the whole does not actually have a higher payoff for the whole group than some sub-coalitions but the distribution is different. This is simply an accidental result of particular numbers here, and since I got the numbers by writing some down at random, and making a few revisions to get the example to work, there is no evidence that this is the way things are in the real world.

Before we turn to more complex arrangements, let us consider some of the problems. The numbers I have put down are preference weights of the individuals, and we never have any real information about this. The individual himself can cardinalize his preferences over a set of three alternatives, or a set of coalitions, but the outsider cannot. Further, the other members of the potential coalitions do not know the value of a given alternative to any particular party.

In this particular case with only three people voting and choosing among three alternatives, it is not improbable, following the argument of David Hume's meadow,[2] that the parties could make pretty good guesses as to the other parties' value of the various alternatives. They would be guesses, of course, and there is no reason to believe that they would turn out to be correct in all cases.

When we turn to larger numbers of people choosing among more alternatives, this lack of information is very important. All of this indicates that in bargaining in actual legislature that kind of talent that helps a man win at poker is of great value. In poker there is no need to try and convince other people that you personally are honest and sincere. Log-rolling is different.

Lyndon Johnson, or for that matter our recent Republican presidential candidate, Dole, was extremely good at this kind of bargaining; making up coalitions among other people in which they must weigh the relative preferences they have for various combinations of bills. To say that they are extremely good does not mean that they are even close to perfect. A lot of errors are to be expected.

Further it should be noted that strictly speaking none of these coalitions dominate any of the others except that all of the two party coalitions from the standpoint of those two parties dominate the Paretian outcome. Once again referring back to earlier work, that was also true in the log-rolling road model.

At this point I would like to switch to a larger model rather similar to that shown in Tables 7.1 and 7.2, but with more voters and more alternatives. Unfortunately, as I pointed out before, this in essence is impractical. Under the circumstances I am forced to use verbal, rather general terms to discuss the situation. I believe that what I am about to say is as rigorous as a numerical set running over a small library even if it is not quite so impressive in appearance.

Think of a considerable number of people who are using simple majority voting, and have a considerable number of alternatives which they can consider. Note that any one of these people can add another alternative or so to the pot, if he thinks that he can gain from it, so in essence the number of alternatives which are available at least theoretically is much in excess of the number of the representatives.

We continue with the realistic assumption that although each individual is capable of cardinalizing his own preference order over all of these real and potential alternatives, he does not actually know what the cardinal values are of the other members of the group. He can make guesses, but they are only guesses. Is the representative from a farming district in Iowa really more interested in the farm program than he is in getting a new post office in his largest city? If he is so interested, by how much?

Obviously the answer to these questions are important in setting up a coalition and equally obviously the representative from Iowa has a fairly strong motive, like a poker player, to prevent the other people from making exact estimates. Perhaps he can get both. If he succeeds in convincing them that although he is indeed in favor of the post office, his preference is relatively weak, he may get two post offices.

What I have said so far does not require any differentiation between the two different kinds of log-rolling described before. Johnson was good at both of them. In general that is characteristic of the legislature except that modern legislatures pass so many bills that a good many provisions like the ones discussed by Stockman actually go in without many people having seen them. Thus there is no direct trade but there is some kind of quota arrangement that keeps too many of these things from going in.

A good deal of log-rolling legislation depends on getting public support. Government activity can and frequently does create externalities, as well as in many cases dealing with a private market externality. In the present agricultural program, the citizens who pay more for their food are the victims of the externality. The externality that is eliminated by this program is that the farmers would be injured if the price were lower as a result of there being no government program.

It is usual in economics to refer to this kind of externality as a 'mere pecuniary externality.' Why we use that term I do not know. In any event, most economists, including myself feel that this kind of externality should not be the source of government action, but most of us know that it is. That government action may create both pecuniary and the classical kind of externality is unfortunate, but the world is in many ways an unsatisfactory place.

We can take the farm program as a very simple case. In the first place it is likely that individual farm representatives and for that matter individual groups of farmers are more interested in some crops than in others. There are a good many aspects of the farm program which substantially every farmer and substantially every Congressman from an agricultural district favors. In this case it is a question of making up a package of units in which this collection of things is matched with things in other fields with the result that people on the whole are in favor of it or do not know that it exists.

You must keep in mind that the Congressman must be reelected. To repeat a very old aphorism, 'In order to be a great senator one must first of all be a senator.' An act attracting support through log-rolling almost of a necessity takes the form of a long bill with a large number of special provisions in it.

This is being written right after a presidential election. I do not think that anybody paid a great deal of attention to the formal platforms of the parties. Indeed both presidential candidates said publicly that they have not read them. Still, the candidates produced in their speeches a bundle of political proposals on which they hoped that they would gain. These are examples of complex log-rolling bargaining in which an appeal is made to millions of people with each and every provision, but they are not the same million as you move from one to another.

I realize that there is a great deal of simple personality involved in this kind of campaigning. Clinton claimed that Dole was irresponsible in offering to balance the budget and cut taxes. Dole did not specifically called Clinton a crook, but a number of public opinion polls indicate that although a majority of the populace of the United States favored Clinton over Dole, a somewhat larger majority of Americans thought that Clinton was a crook.

The voters have to weigh judgements of personal integrity, intelligence, and so on, against specific promises that politicians make. The voter realizes that he does not know all the specific promises and does know that a good many of them will probably not be carried out. The last is not a statement that they are deliberately making false promises, but that the situation as it develops may make it impossible for the winner to carry out things that they have promised.

The situation here is complicated and as a matter of fact, empirical research has not been very helpful. It has been possible to demonstrate that there is some connection between special interest pressure and the passage of bills. These tests are difficult because if somebody from a farm state is observed to vote against some provision that will in fact benefit his state, you do not know if he has been paid off for this vote elsewhere. Thus the empirical tests look at only part of the results of these bargains and hence have a very large error component.

It does appear true that congressmen usually vote in accordance with the issues favored by their constituents and where they do not, they have a tendency to be beaten. It is true that Congressmen like the rest of us are sometimes willing to take sacrifices for the public goods or to help the poor, and sometimes will vote against the interest of their constituents even if they are aware of the fact this may lead to their losing an election. It is even possible that the constituents will reward them for doing something which injures the constituents but looks morally justified.

Thus we can see that the log-rolling problem is extremely complex, requires difficult calculations, which difficult as they are by no means are obviously correct and may lead to unintentional consequences.

The original civil liberties act was opposed by Judge Smith, the head of House Rules Committee, and as a sort of joke he stuck women in as another group that would be protected. It seems likely that he thought this would be easily voted out of the legislation or, preferably, it would kill the whole bill. As it turned out this joke of Judge Smith was the most important part of the bill. Far more people were affected by it than by the remainder of the bill. This was a completely unconscious bit of log-rolling by a man who was an extremely competent and experienced performer in the area.

It is obviously impossible for say 435 congressmen, or the 600 plus members of the Vermont legislature to make complex individual bargains with each other. It is necessary to some extent to centralize the bargaining procedure. Some time ago there was a book written which alleged that in the early part of the 18th century the organization of bargaining procedure was essentially by way of the particular boarding houses that congressmen stayed in when they went to Washington. This was disproved by further research.[3] Still, it was not improbable.

The easiest place to study the matter is the British House of Commons. In most of in this century there was a very strict and firm party discipline. Presumably the reason for this party discipline was the party control of almost all resources that could be used in campaigning. In a mild way this control has been breaking down recently mainly because the balance between the parties is so extremely close that the Conservative prime minister did not dare to throw people out for violating orders.

In this case there is no doubt that the bargaining that goes on is actually performed in the cabinet. It is true that the individual ministers, and to some extent the civil servants that work with them, bargain among themselves.[4] In practice, however, civil servants do not have the power and deviousness of Sir Humphrey Appleby, and the cabinet ministers are not bunglers like the Honorable James Hacker.

It is clear that much the same kind of thing comes out of the Houses of Parliament as comes out of our legislature. Further, the concern for the next election with careful examination of pressure groups and the like is equivalent. The only difference is that in their case there is a far more efficient method of making the bargains. Further, in their case because the party has such control over the individual members of parliament, bargains are simpler and normally point to things that are expected to effect the entire next election.

In the United States they very frequently turn on matters which will not effect the election as a whole, but will effect somebody form the Third District of Illinois. The vast collection of very narrow special provisions described by Stockman is much less characteristic of the House of Commons.

It should be kept in mind that this is only an approximately correct description of the House of Commons. The cabinet not only has to worry about whether it is getting help at the next election, it has to worry about whether it can get it through the House of Lords. The House of Lords is the mere shadow of what it used to be, and further, it is no longer overwhelmingly hereditary. There are a lot of people who have been appointed to it by the Prime Minister of the day, and remain members until such time as they die.[5] It does not have a complete veto. But it can impose considerable delays and inconvenience on the government of the day if a majority of the Lords object to some bill.

Further, 'majority' of the Lords is in itself a work of art. The number of Lords is very large, and only a fairly small minority of them actually turn up for its deliberations. Something that excites 'country members' so that they come up could cause great difficulties. Thus the bargain made up must contain not just the members of the commons, but at least something for the Lords.

The second place that we will look at is more complicated than the English House of Commons, but not anywhere near as complicated as the American House of Representatives. This is in countries where what is called proportional representation in Europe is applied.[6] This is practiced in its pure form in Israel and The Netherlands. Since Israel gets a good deal more attention in the American press than The Netherlands, let us talk about that.

Once again the party discipline there is very strict, although it is possible for an individual to simply leave his party if he wishes. The voting method is one which a party puts up a list, and people then vote for the party and the party gets, let us say 20 percent of the seats in the legislature if it has twenty percent of the vote. These seats are awarded by starting at the top of the list submitted by the party and running down until they reach 20 percent of the Knesset.

The party organization determines where the name of the candidate will be on the list, and troublemakers will be put far enough down so that they never get elected. It is possible to quit and start your own party and people do from time to time. Since the method permits tiny parties to continue to exist, this is not as hopeless as you might expect.[7]

The result of this is that there is a number of small parties, and particularly religious parties. The Arabs are so badly organized politically that they do not mean much. There are also occasional small parties formed by members of the major parties who have moved out. As a general rule, all of these parties have policies which are made up within the party not by the kind of log-rolling I have described above, but the organization at the top which decides who will occupy the seats. They will then have to form a coalition government with the other parties. Normally the coalition consists of one of the two major parties Labor of Likud together with a number of religious orthodox parties. The orthodox parties seem mainly to be interested in straightforward pork, in the way of payments for religious schools, etc., but they have feelings about religious matters; the rules that say that you cannot drive in certain areas on Saturday, that you must wear a hat when you enter certain areas, etc.

This system means that individuals attempting to exert personal influence must first go to their party leadership, which is quite different from the system in the United States. Occasionally there are votes in which people are told to vote their conscience, but this is an unusual phenomenon. Log-rolling negotiation then takes place among the parties, and the religious parties, by threatening to change over to the other large party from the one that they are currently in coalition with, have very great leverage.

Of course, the party leadership are members of the cabinet, so this is somewhat like the situation in England. In any event, you can put your fingers on who organizes substantially all coalitions. Both of these systems are simple compared with that which we observe in the United States, particularly in the House of Representatives, or in the various American State legislatures. Sometimes with cabinet government it can be much more complex. France until de Gaulle's reforms and Italy for a very long time had almost rotating cabinets.

In this case the log-rolling negotiations were still carried out by the parties, but the current cabinet ministers do not have any clear ideas whether they will be in the same position tomorrow. Even so, the actual log-rolling bargains were made in a rather centralized manner because of the comparative strength of the parties. Extreme decentralization as in the American system is unusual. In our case it comes from the weak party discipline which in turn comes from the fact that the party has few tools to punish deviant members. People frequently regard descriptions of this kind of thing as actually an attack on the system. I am not wildly enthusiastic about it, but it is not something that we need to worry about terribly. In public finance theory you get the impression that the point of government is the internalization of externalities. We have something like, let us say, the weather bureau, which benefits the whole United States, but where no one would, by and of themselves, be willing to pay for it. We therefore turn to the government and in this case the national government.[8] Of course the government weather bureau also generates negative externalities for those who do not want to pay taxes for such a purpose.

Many things which have externalities, however, have strictly limited short-range externalities. I mentioned post offices and traditionally, although not today so much, that was one of the major sources of political pork. Clearly putting it somewhere benefits people only in its immediate vicinity and injures everyone else that has to pay taxes, except in so far as the location might possibly improve the efficiency with which mail is delivered.

It probably would be most efficient if we could somehow or another provide a set of narrow voting constituencies concerning only those people who benefit and lose from a given act. This would require literally thousands and thousands of separate jurisdictions and is too complicated. Our present system involves trades, sometimes in the state or local government.

Through log-rolling something with a rather restricted area of influence is provided by a larger government in return for putting something of similar restricted interest elsewhere. This cannot be objected to, although it is not entirely optimal. It does greatly simplify the voters problem. They only have to vote on a relatively few officials.[9]

The basic problem here is, if we go back to the road model and assume that it is not perfectly symmetrical as it is there, that with simple majority voting you get a considerable amount of investment in these local public projects. If the people who vote on them are representatives who are themselves elected by simple majority vote, you may have as little as one-quarter actually benefitting and therefore have something like four times as much of whatever is provided as would be optimal. This is inefficient and both Professor Buchanan and I and a number of other people think that the voting majority should be increased. Note that this inefficiency does not come form log-rolling, it comes from the voting rule. Further, our actual procedures require more than a majority, although not enough.

Without log-rolling either these things would not be provided at all, or in any event, only those which directly advantaged one-quarter of the populace would be put through and could inflict injury on the remaining 75 percent. Increasing the required majority is one remedy.

It should be repeated here that we in the United States are not accustomed to simple majority voting as I pointed out several times before. A bill requires a majority in the House, but sixty percent of the actual members of the Senate if it is thought to be important. It also needs the president's approval. If the president does not approve it requires two-thirds in both houses. This is undoubtedly much more efficient than the simple majority vote that we see in places like Israel.

Personally, I favor one house elected by proportional representation, and the other by the English first past the post system that we use. The argument is that this would be equivalent to having two radically different legislatures, and a majority in both would be equivalent to considerably more than a majority in a single house legislature.

There is the fact that the minorities would get at least one representative in the house that is proportionally elected, and the geographical areas would continue to be represented as they are now. It would probably be wise to elect the president by another method than either of those. The one we now use is inefficient, but there is a wide choice of these and I shall not select one here.

All of this does not eliminate log-rolling, but it simply requires that the coalitions to get something would be both larger and more diverse than in our present legislature. This should make it harder to get things passed which are supported by a bare majority of voters in a bare majority of the constituencies.

It should reduce the number of log-rolling coalitions that are put through, but the ones that would be cut are the ones where the total benefit is markedly less than the total cost. Going back to our road model, if we required a 75 percent majority then people deciding to repair roads, and setting up coalitions for that purpose, would have to take into account 75 percent of the costs. This would mean that many log-rolling coalitions to repair roads would be eliminated, but these would be the ones where the cost is less than 75 percent of the actual social costs.

This may seem a modest goal. What we would like is to get governments to do things that are Pareto optimal and nothing else. As a matter of fact we cannot do this and if one thinks carefully about the market he quickly realize that we do not have that in the market either. The reason that we do not have it in the market is quite simply that the combination of the imperfections of the property institutions together with transactions costs mean that not everything is taken into account.

What we should do is select those institutions which over the long-run and granting many different transactions, accepting that we will sometimes be on one side and sometimes on the other gives us the highest present discounted value. This means that any of these transactions, voting or the in market, looked at just by itself without the general pattern will turn out to be non-pareto optimal.

The original decision to adopt a general set of institutions with this characteristic may, however, be pareto optimal. It may literally be the best thing for everyone even though the individual transactions that are taking place after that agreement could be improved upon if we were not concerned with transaction costs and if everyone concerned had a veto power over the agreement. In the real-world we will be compelled to use log-rolling and not to require unanimity because the costs of unanimity are just too great. We consciously accept the probability of having difficulties from time to time on individual transactions because we feel that the entire collection of such transactions give us a better deal than would with another set of institutions.

This does not of course indicate that the present set of institutions is ideal. Indeed as the reader probably knows I am a fairly radical reformer. Reform however should not aim at pareto optimality in each transaction. It should simply aim at a set of institutions which over the long-run and over many transactions will give people as good a return as is possible.

---

1 It should be remembered that in the United States party discipline is weak, and when we speak of the party we should more accurately speak of a considerable part of the party.

2 Hume said that two owners of a meadow could easily reach agreement on draining a meadow. With many owners this would be very difficult.

3 I am not giving the name of the young political scientist that made the original error or attacks on him. It was an honest mistake and an easy one to make.

4 *The Complete Yes Minister*, and *The Complete Yes Prime Minister*, are delightful books, and the television programs were equally delightful. Further, there is an element of truth in them.

5   Australia and Canada have a sort of copy of this in which there is no hereditary component.

6   This will be much more fully described later.

7   Some time ago a man who was under indictment for various crimes started his own party, campaigned vigorously, and was elected to the Knesset with enough votes so if he only put his wife in as a candidate she would have been elected too. This made him immune to arrest.

8   Since similar activity is carried out in Europe with a lot of countries, many of which are smaller than our states, it is not clear that it has to be national, but that is the domain for the current discussion.

9   See my *The New Federalist*, Vancouver: Frazer Institute (1994), for further discussion of this point.

CHAPTER 8
Efficiency in Log-Rolling

The very meaning of 'efficiency' when we deal with log-rolling requires some explanation. It is clear that government actions are rarely Pareto optimal. Some people are injured and receive no direct compensation for that injury. An obvious case of this is the victim of a war, but there are many less dramatic examples. At the moment in Tucson we are having a radio telephone arrangement using very short wavelengths installed and this requires that the transmitters and receivers be at considerable height above the ground. They are putting up towers, which personally, I think are inoffensive, but certainly are not beautiful. A number of people are complaining. Nothing will be done about these complaints except that they may get a visit from some plausible representative of the telephone company who will try to soothe them.

There are many others examples such as the farm program and the Washington Metro system, which is heavily subsidized by people who never use it. An example which got a great deal of publicity was the federal government subsidization of certain 'art' objects created by Maplethorp. This is particularly interesting because no subsidy was necessary. He is a moderately wealthy man as a result of selling various of his productions. He surely could have sold these objects, or if he felt in the mood made a contribution. The government sponsorship irritated an awful lot of people who were not compensated.

What we actually mean when we talk about government efficiency is efficiency over the long run, that is, we want the government on the whole to give people the best bargain that is possible granted the existence of transaction costs and the impossibility of getting everyone's agreement to all projects. I have at various times referred to this as Pareto optimality in the large. This would mean that there is no arrangement which would give everyone a better deal.

Most people who talk about government being efficient or, more commonly, inefficient, do not define what they mean. The question of whether log-rolling is or is not efficient is even more difficult This makes claims made by some scholars that log-rolling is not efficient hard to evaluate.

People who make such claims are mainly proponents of democracy and democracy everywhere functions by way of log-rolling. Nor is there any way to get rid of it. I should say also that something very similar to log-rolling appears in non-democratic governments, so in a way it is simple a characteristic of governments *per se*.

Some governments consciously inflict injury on some people in order to benefit others. In some cases the group that benefited is the majority. In others the immediate family of the House of Medici. We should not, however, assume that governments are often motivated by a positive desire to injure people, indeed frequently governmental officials are consciously trying to help. Nevertheless, they must know that some people are injured and there is no way of helping A, B and C without injuring D.

There has been some debate in the literature about whether log-rolling is or is not a contribution to efficiency. In the *Calculus of Consent*[1] Buchanan and I said that it was, but there are various people who have objected. There was an actual debate, not of great length in the American Political Science Review in which William

Riker and W.E. Brams argued that it was inefficient, giving an example in which log-rolling apparently led to an outcome that was for all parties inferior.

I responded rather weakly. [2] The reason for the weakness in my response was that Peter Ordeshook orally told me that Riker and Brams had simply chosen the wrong log rolling bargain. There was another coalition that had paid off very well. I confirmed this but did not mention it in my response because I thought it belonged to Peter Ordeshook. Later I heard that he, a student of Riker, did not want to use it and had hoped that I would. Under the circumstances, the Riker and Brams paper has not been demolished as it should be.

As far as I know this is the only real argument that rent-seeking is inefficient, but we have not done very much to indicate that it is efficient. I would like to take up this issue here.

To begin with let us consider the efficiency of ordinary bargaining. I bought a house not very long ago, and this was the third time that I had done so. The housing market is normally referred to as a well-organized market, although there are certain cartel aspects to it. What happened was that a real estate lady and I looked at a number of houses, discussed the price, made an offer (traditionally) 15 percent under the asking price, had difficulty with the seller, and eventually got it.

There are two possible inefficiencies, one of which is the need to use a real estate lady, but I was going to a totally strange city, and I must say she was remarkably good at figuring out my preferences on just a brief acquaintance. Still, it seems likely there were other houses available in Tucson which both in price and amenities would have suited me better. I stopped my search without having exhausted the market, which is what every shopper does.

We do not normally regard this as inefficient, but it does mean that the distribution of resources and other things in the society is not really perfect as seen from God's eye. We all spend limited time in search, and the bargaining process is not perfect, etc.

Nevertheless, no one will regard this as an inefficient market even though it is not one that is divinely perfect.

My reason for bringing this up is that it will turn out to be true in log-rolling also. But there is another problem with the private market. If having bought my house I proceeded to paint it purple, because I like purple, I would have been afflicting a cost on my neighbors. Perhaps a significance cost, if they were hoping to sell their own house at a good price.

This is one of the straightforward externalities that we are not at all surprised by when we find them in the private market. When I buy a house I take into account what I might need and what the man who is selling it to me considers his needs.[3] We do not directly worry about what other people might be affected by the transactions. As the reader no doubt knows, there are various rules about housing, zoning, structure, etc., which are intended to deal with those, but these are all government activities, not part of the private market.[4]

The outcome of the market process in the real world, even a very well-functioning marketing process, is one in which there is not a perfect match in the sense that each buyer gets the ideal product for his price, and each seller sells it to the best buyer, nor that the transaction covers all of the effects of the transaction. As we shall see log-rolling has the same negative characteristics.

Suppose I want some change in the law. First, just wanting the change does not do me any good. Let us assume there are other people who will agree with me that this change is desirable, but by ourselves we are not numerous enough to get it through. In other words there are people who do not want the change.

If there is no log-rolling, we would simply count the heads, and if there is a majority on one side that would get it. Note, firstly, it is not obvious that the level of intensity of the wants on either side is the same, and secondly, it may well be that the people who will be injured by the law being passed are in favor of something else and could be readily compensated by an agreement.

If we were trying to maximize the wellbeing of the world we would like a system in which externalities, injuries inflicted on people who are not included in the agreement, are taken care of. If my neighbor wants to paint his house purple, it does indeed lower the value of my block. The fact he got a number of his friends to agree that his house could be painted purple, (preferably friends who live some distance away), would not mean I do not suffer an externality. I would be injured even if a vote put through by the relevant constituency said he could do so.

The fact that government actions can create externalities, just as well as eliminating them, is almost unknown to most economists. Why this is so is very difficult to say. It is obvious when you think about the matter. It is indeed possible for a government to inflict great externalities. There were a number of citizens in Baghdad, a short time ago, who suddenly discovered that they were suffering from fairly severe externalities from the actions of a democratic government.

We do not have to look internationally for this kind of thing. There are many laws enacted by legislatures which are strongly opposed by some of their own citizens. I can be as much, or more, injured if a majority of my neighbors vote in something I object to as I would be by offensive private action. Both impose externalities.

Let me go back to the case used by Douglas Rae to criticize the super majority requirement.[5] The reader will recall this concerned a railroad car back in the days when smoking was perfectly legal in such places, and some of the passengers wanted to smoke, and others did not want them to smoke. Rae argued under this circumstance the simple majority vote is ideal. Of course, this assumes as I mentioned before that the intensity of the preference of the two groups is the same, which is not obviously so.

Suppose we put in the equivalent of log-rolling. We say that you can make trades on other issues, then even if it turned out that only a small minority wanted smoking discontinued, they could simply offer a joint motion, that (i) smoking shall be discontinued and (ii) that they will buy a 'free beer' for all the other people. This is a clear-cut log-rolling transaction and would no doubt get through if the trip was going to be fairly short. If it was going to long you might need several beers.

Turning from the Rae example, generally speaking things that are suggested for vote fall into two categories. Firstly, they are things that will benefit or possibly prevent injury to a fairly small group, and this is a fairly large benefit of injury, and will cost the rest a small amount of money per head. As you will recall on Table 7.1, I had a set of preferences for 3 voters, and explained that we would think of them as preferences for 3 schools, in 3 distinct parts of the city.

Presumably, on a completely uncompensated vote for each of the schools, they would not be built because in each case the people who had to pay the taxes would be more numerous than the people who would benefit from the school. On the other hand, it is fairly obvious that compensation in that case, other schools, in other parts of the City, could get it through.

What we would like is a system that does two things: firstly, it prevents things which actually inflict more injury than gain from going through. As we will see this consideration is not strictly speaking possible, but we can limit the maximum loss inflicted.

Secondly, we would like everybody to be treated well. For example, I would regard providing the mug of 'free beer' to people who are prevented from smoking, although they would like to do so, as a better arrangement than just preventing them from smoking. In this case the decision for smoking or non-smoking is a general one, and does not provide specialized benefits, or prevent specialized injury to a small minority, but still I would argue that it is sensible to compensate, if we can.

In cases where the beneficiaries of the bill or the particular project are a small minority, but where the benefit to them is greater than the total cost we would like to have that get through and, other than a possible charitable motive on the part of the majority, the only way of doing so is compensation. We can put together a bundle of such proposals so that a majority will benefit from the entire bundle. Or we can vote on them one at a time with people agreeing to vote for a friend's position, if he votes for them. As far as I can see there is no significant difference between them. It is fairly clear log-rolling can generate a benefit. As a matter of fact people who are engaged in legislative process know this, and engage in log-rolling. They seem to do it in a somewhat bad conscience, however. Those who object to log-rolling are simply objecting to it because they have not thought about the matter very much. The examples they use against log-rolling are like the one Douglas Rae used in which their is a simple majority and nobody is much injured. It should be noted that even in that case the minority, if it feels strongly, may be able by compensation to get its preference.

Long ago when Buchanan and I were working on *The Calculus of Consent* we discussed the situation of the Jews in Germany. If there had been a well functioning democratic legislature, it seems fairly certain that the Jews by trading their votes for a number of other projects could have prevented severe discrimination against themselves even if the majority of those in Germany favored it because they would not favor it enough so that they would not accept compensation.

To look back to an American example, Booker T. Washington was a man who did a great deal for his race, although it is not popular right now to say so. The Tuskegee Institute, which he founded, depended very heavily on the payments that he received from a white dominated state legislature. It seems fairly certain that this was the result of a trade in which he used what political power he had to support that group on some things, and they responded by supporting the Institute. Once again the trade was not only good for Booker T. Washington, but no doubt good for his race.

There are two arguments for compensating the minority for its loss. The first of these is sort of an equity argument, although I believe there are many people whose moral code does not support it. Nevertheless, it is clear that people can be badly injured by government action, and compensating them is at least nice, if not morally required.

The second argument is one of efficiency. To repeat what we have said before, there are many government activities which benefit only a minority, but where the cost is spread over a larger group. There are also cases where the opposite happens, where the action removes an injury to the minority once again at a minor cost to a larger group. With pure majority voting with everybody simply voting for their preference on each issue these could not get through, and most people would agree that it is desirable they do so.

I should say here that there is another way for dealing with these matters. We could set up specialized small constituencies for each of these issues and put the tax entirely upon that small constituency. Unfortunately, as a general solution, this is impractical although clearly in some cases it can be done. It would be nice to try it when we could.

Returning to the main theme; getting through these many minor projects by grouping them together with other projects either in the form of one bill, as in the bond issue, I have continuously referred to in Tucson or by making trades on several bills, clearly permits them to be passed when it would not be possible otherwise.

Is this actually efficient? If it is efficient is the simple majority rule the best bet? There are other possibilities. We could permit any small minority to have one project of its own, with every minority being included. I doubt many of my readers will favor that approach.

The standard procedure which is to hold a vote on it does raise immediately the question of what kind of vote. If we look at the American constitution there are many cases in which the answer to that is something more than a majority. Getting a bill through both houses of Congress, with the two houses being elected differently, and then having the President sign it into legislation, or sending it back and having it win by a two–thirds majority in both houses is clearly something more than a simple majority.

A number of states, including Arizona, have recently been passing constitutional amendments which require more than a simple majority for various matters, mainly tax increases. Finland actually requires an 80 percent majority for a tax increase. Some time ago, Jack Goode and I[6] suggested requiring a two-thirds majority in the Supreme court to establish a precedent.[7] Whether you agree with this or not it is clearly a possibility. Juries, after all, vote unanimously. Is this more or less efficient? If we have a single issue upon which some people are in favor of a particular action, and some oppose, and we have good reason to believe that the intensity of their preferences are about the same, one can make an argument for simple majority voting. Note those conditions. It has to be a simple yes or no choice, and the preferences for people on both sides have to be roughly the same, and in particular, we are not interested in compensating the people who are injured for their injuries. These are very strict conditions and probably seldom met.

If we are going to engage in log-rolling, and to repeat, it is something that every one knows is the basic way in which modern democratic governments operate, then the arguments for using more than a simple majority in order to pass bills are strong. Suppose we can, by making up a log-rolling bargain, get a majority of the vote while injuring 49 percent of the population. It is essential for this to work through that the total benefit which is generated by this bill be at least 51 percent of its total costs preferably more.

If we go up to requiring a two–thirds majority the benefit necessary to log-roll the thing through is at least 66.66 percent of the cost. The reader will recall that this was demonstrated in the simplified road model given earlier.

So far we have not talked about voting to prevent something going through. Suppose that Hitler had acquired power in Germany, but not dictatorial power. In other words he had to get things through the legislature[8]. Then suppose that a majority of the population were anti-Semitic, although whether they wanted to kill was another matter. Perhaps their attitude was not much stronger than in my home town of Rockford, Illinois in the 1930s. There was minor social discrimination against the Jews, but nothing serious. Under these circumstances, the Jews by making a significant log rolling offer could no doubt get the bill weakened or even stopped.

This is an extreme example, but in general log-rolling works both ways. A promise to some group to give them a special bill in return for their vote for something I want can be countered by someone on the other side promising a gift in return for a vote against my bill.

As a result of this, in general, it will normally not be possible for a log-rolling coalition to inflict serious injury upon sizeable minorities. If we did not have log-rolling that could be perfectly possible, and fairly easy to find many examples other than the Jewish one which I gave above.

For a long time now the tobacco interests have been able to follow this technique to prevent what is a clearly the majority from bringing in anti-tobacco legislation. It is a slow and desperate guerilla war, and they are slowly losing, but they have been able to hold it off for a considerable time.

My readers may think that this is unfortunate, but it is true in this case legislation which would badly injure a minority has been bought off by log-rolling agreements mainly entered into by the representatives from the tobacco states. The same kind of thing can be said with respect to the various efforts to get rid of the agricultural farm subsidy program. The final act which was passed by Gingrich and his friends arranged that it would be gradually eliminated, and here again we have a set of bills in which an overwhelming majority would benefit, but which would remove a considerable subsidy to a minority.[9]

These have been simple examples. Let us think about the matter more generally. Suppose that in society there are possible various changes in the status quo to benefit some people, and in general they would injure some other people. There is an ideal way to deal with this problem which is unfortunately impossible, We could assess the gain and loss to everyone. If the gain is greater than the loss take the action and assess the winners to compensate the losers. Contrary wise, if the loss was greater than the gain, the change would not be made.

There might be some who would suggest under these circumstances the winners from the inaction be assessed in order to compensate those who should benefit from the change. Granted the number of possible changes in the status quo I doubt that even in the impractical universe where the first proposal was feasible that this would be.

We do like people who lose from any given transaction to be compensated, but more important we want to make sure that on the whole the gains from various transactions are greater than the loss. This is obviously true in my effort to buy a house. We have been reading about the situation in Bosnia in which people got houses without paying for them, and I take it that we all think that is a bad idea.

Much of economics has been devoted to discussions of the way in which private transactions can be structured so that the gains will normally more than balance the losses, and in general we hope that nobody will be injured very much. We should do the same in politics.

We do not require in the private market that everybody who is affected by the transaction be compensated. We do not give all of them the right to veto transactions, unless they are so compensated. We should also not give a complete veto to anybody injured in politics. The reason is the same in both cases. In both cases this would provide an unfortunately strong bargaining position for many small groups. I could maintain that the sale of one of the houses in my homeowners' association[10]injured me and demand compensation. Essentially I could attempt to obtain the whole of the benefit of the bargain for myself.

The fact that people who do have a veto right may do just this is the reason that land assembly for large projects is so difficult. The hold outs gain more than the people who are cooperative and everyone is motivated to hold out. The same would be true in politics.

Let us temporarily ignore these problems and assume that we have an infinite amount of time to make any political change. To repeat, it is not a reasonable condition but it makes it easier to talk about the matter. In these circumstances everybody would have to be compensated, and the end project would in fact not injure any one, and the gains would be distributed among the interested parties. The problem, of course, is the infinite time which, in the real world, would be extremely costly. In fact, it is an impossible system.

Note here that compensation for everything except the transaction cost would be complete. Leaving aside the (tremendous) transaction cost, projects in which the gain is greater than the loss could be got through and the society as a whole would gain from these projects but so would each individual, or at least none of them would be injured. The moment we go down from requiring unanimity these two conditions cease to be true. On the other hand, transactions cost shrinks.

Once again this is true in the private market. If we permitted anyone who felt they were in any way injured by any given transaction to veto it, this would provide that no one was injured, and the externalities are eliminated, but all agree that the cost of introducing this type of bargaining is greater than the gain.

In the private market what we try to do is to see to it that the people who might be injured in a major way by a given change in ownership are compensated. The major person injured if I move into my present house without paying for it would be the previous owner, as so many Bosnians have discovered, but our laws will see to it that he is compensated. People who suffer less are normally not compensated.

In politics, oddly enough, we would not do this if there were no log-rolling. Log-rolling does move in the general direction of compensating the losers, and moves in that general direction more strongly if the requirement for the vote is greater than a simple majority.

Let us consider how log-rolling does work. The first thing to be said is that the provisions that are brought up for discussion in general will be those in which it is thought that the gains from those who win is great enough so that they can compensate at least some of the losers. The number of the losers must be compensated is a product of the voting rule.

In the market it is possible that there are transactions when the purchase of something may actually be socially negative because the people who are not permitted to veto it are injured more than the buyer and seller gain, but that is presumably rare. In politics if we use simple majority voting it is not all obvious that this would be rare.,

We can easily put our finger on projects like the farm program mentioned above, protective tariffs, the Washington Metro System,[11] which violate this condition. With a higher majority the cost would be closer to the benefit. Still, all three examples I gave above were enacted by our present national system which implicitly is fairly close to a two–thirds majority.

The fact that these bills can be got through is evidence that our present system is not perfect but nobody thinks it is. Once again I refer to the analogy of the real estate market. The outcome there is not perfect either but granted the cost imposed by putting additional requirements on, it is better than we could expect if we did not have such transactions.

Let me make a suggestion of a change in the real estate market which is not intended seriously but which has something to with do the proposal that the majorities be more than simple majority. Suppose that each lot which is to be sold, can be sold only if the owners of all the other lots which adjoin it give their consent.[12] I take it that the readers would all agree that the cost of such a system would exceed the benefit, although it would guarantee that certain externalities, i.e., the cost to a neighbor by the sale of a house to somebody that he detests would be eliminated.

This is a case in many ways like the voting case we have given. In both cases some kind of arrangement under which we balance the reduction of externalities by requiring larger numbers of people to consent against the transaction cost which that would generate. In both cases the outcome cannot be made perfectly efficient, but we can hope for reasonable efficiency.

It is not normally noted but in addition to the people who are setting up the log-rolling bargain for a given bill there are people who will be injured by it and are not going to be compensated and they will be attempting to set up another coalition either to simply eliminate this from consideration in favor of another basic proposal, or at least beat it. Thus, as in the real estate market, you have bargaining with two parties involved, and there are more than two parties.

The outcome is presumably reasonably but not perfectly efficient. In this case when we say that it is reasonably efficient in the political arena we are conceding that there may be some people in the minority who are very badly injured. Nevertheless, it is efficient in the sense that there is no other coalition put together which can beat it.

This is one of the basic reasons that we do not see cycling in the real world. I earlier remarked when talking about the paradox of voting that one of the reasons it does not seem to have remained in the center of thought on politics is it is very hard to find any examples of it actually occurring. The fact that these bargains are not dominated explains this. In our example before we had A, B, and C in a cycle. If it is A, plus two post offices, then it is likely that A will be voted in and will turn out to be stable.

This is not proof that it is desirable because the people who wanted C, may in fact be opposed to A very strongly, but not in any need of post offices. Under the circumstances, they will be left in the uncompensated minority.

The net result of this is that the final bargain that comes through is as we have said quite stable. It is not terribly well known but it is true that the higher the required majority the less likely there will be cycling. That does not mean it is impossible with any majority you care to name, but it requires fairly stringent restrictions on the shape of the different curves, etc. as the majority requirements goes up.

The end product is that log-rolling which is dominant in all democratic societies[13] leads to outcomes that are efficient in the same sense that market outcomes are efficient. This is efficiency within the constraints of the system. It is easier to restrict externalities in the market than it is in politics.

This is probably true because the existing literature on democratic government rather assumes that we have majority voting and we normally do have voting which is not wildly different from majority. The example that I gave above of an 80 percent majority for tax increases in Finland is rare. Normally you will have something like the British House of Commons and Lords, which is almost pure majority voting or like the American complex system[14] which is equivalent to somewhere around a 60 to 66 percent majority in a single house.

Both of these permit significant negative externalities to be inflicted on numbers of people and are less efficient in that sense than in a regular market in which we have better transaction laws. To say that they are less efficient than the market is not to say that they are basically inefficient. It is that we could do much better.

We terminate here the main text of this book. We have a system that works but not until fairly recently subject to any kind of scientific analysis. It certainly could be improved upon. Indeed, for myself, I would like to have somebody invent a totally new form of government although I am not positive that this could be done. Nevertheless, we have a system which we should attempt to improve, and for which improvements are possible. This book has attempted to lay the foundations for such improvements.

---

[1] Tullock, Gordon and James Buchanan. *The Calculus of Consent: Logical Foundations of a Constitutional Democracy.* Ann Arbor: University of Michigan Press (1962).

[2] 'Letter to the Editor,' ('Paradox Lost' comment on Riker-Brams article) *American Political Science Review* 68 (December 1974): 22–3.

[3] Also what the real estate lady needs is taken into account.

[4] As it happens in my case the house that I bought was in a homeowners' association which had been set up originally by a private firm, but even that depended upon courts to enforce its rules.

[5] Tullock, Gordon. 'Comment on Rae's "The Limits of Consensual Decision"', *The American Political Science Review* 69(4) (December, 1975): 1295–97.

[6] Suggested that the Supreme Court cases should only be regarded as precedence if at least two–thirds of the Justices agreed with the decision.

[7] A simple majority would decide the instant case, but not set a precedent.

[8] In fact that is how he started, but he converted to dictatorship with great speed.

9 I should say that I am in favor of inflicting this injury on this particular minority because the cost to the average citizen is very much larger than the benefit.

10 Or for that matter the sale of a house in Washington, D.C.

11 It is not widely known, but the fares on Metro pay only a small part of its costs. They do not even pay its operating costs, let alone the capital cost.

12 If the owner proposes a use of the lot which would violate the zoning code, then a variance must be obtained. This normally requires consent of eighty percent of the people in the immediate vicinity.

13 As a matter of fact, it is dominant in dictatorial societies, but takes a different form.

14 We have in the United States the most Byzantine way of passing laws of any modern democracy.

CHAPTER 9
Directions of Representatives

<u>Governments which are democratic</u> (and democracies are about half of all governments in the world at the moment, which represents the high point in history for democracy), <u>all have some kind of elected body.</u> Some also have an elected chief executive, and many American states have elected judges, but this chapter will begin with legislative bodies.

It should be pointed out that it is not necessary this body be elected. Athens had a council which was selected by lot. The 200 members served on it for one year and were then discharged. Unless they were selected by lot again, they had no further responsibilities.

Many other officials in Athens were selected by lot. The machine that they used to make certain that they were getting a random sample is on exhibit in the Stoa of Atallus for those who are curious. Interesting enough the only officials who were not selected this way were the military commanders. Apparently, the citizens were perfectly willing to depend on people selected by lot for most things. When it came to going to war where they might be killed they selected their generals by other methods.

<u>We keep this method to some extent today in the fact that the voting body in the United States which makes more decisions than</u>

any other, the jury, is selected by lot. It is true that today the attorneys on both sides spend a lot of time trying to adjust the jury so that it is favorable to their particular case, but that is a rather modern change.

Indeed, one of the reforms suggested for the jury as a result of the Simpson case is that we go back to a purely lot-selected jury. As far as I know nobody has suggested that the House of Representatives be selected by lot, but if one watches its performance carefully you begin to think that might conceivably be a good idea.

This is enough discussion of random selection. Let us now turn to cases where a legislature is elected, and for the time being we will ignore the fact that legislatures frequently have two houses, both of which are elected. There are two outstanding exceptions to this, The state of Nebraska has a one-house legislature, and England[1] in which one of the houses is hereditary and now weak. Here we will simply discuss the method of voting for selecting a member of the legislature.

Most of the elections to legislatures in the world today can be divided into two categories. The first descends from England, and is the single member constituency in which each constituency sends one member to Parliament or to the House of Representatives, etc. The other is proportional representation which was invented in the 19th century, and is used at the moment by somewhat more than half of all democracies. In its pure form almost no democracy which descends from the English government, as ours does, depends on it.[2] Apparently the English speakers are more conservative than speakers of other languages.

There are two general methods of proportional representation, the first of which was endorsed by John Stewart Mill, and more recently by Dennis Mueller, in his *Constitutional Democracy*, which is a very recent publication. This is little used in the world today, so I put its description off to the Appendix.

Let us turn to the more widespread, and in my view more sensible, method of running proportional representation. For simplicity, I will discuss the two purest cases: Israel, before its recent constitutional amendment which added a President but retained the system for the legislature; and The Netherlands. In these cases, the various parties put up lists of candidates. The voter votes for the party, then the seats are divided in the legislature in proportion to the number of votes received by each party.

The result here is not absolutely certain because of the fact that the votes do not normally fit exactly and there will be some rounding error. We have such error in the United States as the Alabama paradox demonstrated.[3] There are a number of ways in dealing with the rounding error, none of them have much to be said for them, but none of them make very much difference.

This raises the question of who occupies the seats of a given party. Suppose the socialist party has 17 seats, who occupies them? The answer in these pure systems I have been describing is that each party has filed a list with as many names on it as there are seats in the legislature. The judges of election simply take the top 17 on the list.

Since the party can change the order in which people are on its list, this gives the party machine a great deal of power. The result of this is that the party block in the legislature is normally highly cohesive and well disciplined. We will see shortly that there ways of selecting who shall have the socialist seats which are less party dominated, but for the time being let us stick with the system above described.

The result of this scheme is that the American situation in which each congressman has a constituency and works hard to get things for that constituency is no longer of much importance. Pressure groups become functional pressure groups, although it is quite possible that some functional pressure groups will be geographic. It used to be true that in all of the proportional representation countries there was a strong agricultural party which simply tried to do the best for the farmers.

Normally, today, the number of farmers has fallen enough so that such parties are no longer important, but the parties do present well-organized specific function groups in the society, sometimes this is pretty open. In Switzerland, I once met the man who was head of a machine tool manufacturers association, and a member of the legislature. He informed me that the head of the machine tool union was also a member of the legislature, and that on some matters they would be opposed, and on other matters would form an alliance.

In most cases, proportional representation is connected with cabinet type government, with one of the two houses of the legislature selecting the cabinet. Israel has now decided to have an elected Prime Minister,[4] and one of the results of constitutional reform in France is that they have an elected President. The French elected president is an extremely powerful official. The Israeli Prime Minister will probably not be as powerful.

The normal result of proportional representation is that there are a number of parties represented, and if it is one of those countries where a cabinet has to be formed by the legislature this normally means there is a coalition cabinet.

Anthony Downs, in his first book, said this method was bad because voters when they vote for a given party could not predict exactly what coalition it would enter into, and hence did not know what government they were voting for. This is true in most cases, although there have been situations in which a single party has won a majority in proportional representation, but it is of less importance than the information value of the vote.

The voter does know what his party stands for, and it is much more concrete and definite than what a party in a two-party legislature such as we have stands for. Under these circumstances, he introduces more information as to his preferences in the voting process, and presumably has a better chance of favorably influencing the government.

I shall talk no more here about proportional representation. Let us go to the other system, the single member constituency first past the post procedure. This leads to odd items and according to *The New York Times* of today,[5] in the 1996 national election, the Indian Congress party got 30 percent of the votes, and BJP only 26 percent, but the BJP has almost 50 percent more members of the legislature than the congress party. All of this simply just evens things up. For many years the Congress party regularly got 40 to 45 percent of the vote, and about 80 percent of the seats in the parliament. The real change came after Mrs. Gandhi's dictatorship.

Briefly, what happens in a first past the post single constituency system is that the country is broken up into constituencies, each of which will elect one person to the legislature. There has been a good deal of cheating on the break up, and for a while constituencies had radically different numbers of voters. Now they are frequently drawn with complex borders with the intent of guaranteeing the race or party of the member.

Once one has broken up the nation into constituencies the rest is fairly simple. Candidates run. Assuming the simple English method any one who puts up a modest deposit can have his name on the ballot. As a matter of fact there are normally only three names on the ballot representing the Labour, Liberal Democrat, and Conservative parties, but occasionally other people, particularly people who are anxious for publicity, also get on. There are two or three very minor parties like the Scottish Nationalists.

An election is held and the voters check the name they wish and who has the most votes wins. Very commonly, in present day England, this means that the winner has less than the majority of the votes.

It is interesting that it seems likely that if they had a run off the results would be seriously different. At the moment the Liberal

Democrat party could probably collect the votes of all Labour candidates if it was a run off between the Liberal Democrat candidate and the Conservative, and could collect all the votes of all the Conservative candidates if it was run off between the Labour party and the Liberal Democrats. If it was Labour against Conservative I don't know what the outcome would be, but it is clear that the Liberal Democrat candidate is in most cases the Condorcet choice.

The argument normally offered for this system is that it guarantees a strong government because one of the two parties wins. Since there have been periods in which the dominant party didn't have a majority in the house,[6] it is not clear whether this is correct. In any event, it is by no means clear that we want a strong government. Mencken's remark 'No man's property is safe, the legislature is in session' is one of many points of view about the desirability of firm government.

Probably the most firm single control of any American legislature was in the first year and half of the control of the House of Representatives by Gingrich. As far as I know, almost 90 percent of all political scientists[7] thought this was terrible. It depended upon the much weaker control in the Senate, and the President's veto to produce a divided government instead of a firm government. I do not complain about the political scientists critique, but I do wish they would not change positions vigorously whenever the party in power changes.

So much for the pure technology. The point of this chapter is the control of the voters over their representatives in the legislature, or for that matter the president. Elections are only held rather infrequently. This control can hardly be tight and detailed. The alternative control process, what is called in the constitution, 'petition' we usually refer to as lobbying. This is normally an activity of only a few of the voters, rather than everyone. This is the place where special interests are more powerful.

We begin by talking about the pure electoral effect. The reader should keep in mind that this is really the bottom line. The congressman, lobbyist, and so on, always has in mind that the congressman must win the next election if he is to stay in power. Thus, the lobbyist who is most efficient in dealing with him is somebody who can say that they have a certain amount of influence over the voters. In some countries this is not true because there is possible direct bribery, but in the United States that is rare. In the election process the congressmen, president, and so forth, can depend on the voters being rather badly informed. A striking example of this was shown by the regular Pew poll which is taken after elections. After the 1996 election only 75 percent of the voters said that were well enough informed to choose among the candidates. What the other 25 percent thought they were doing is not clear.

Note this is a self-evaluation, not the result of giving them a short examination. They probably claimed a higher level of information by a wide margin than such an examination would show.[8]

Nevertheless voters have a sort of general view of what is going on as a result of exposure to television, newspapers, and other media. Normally they do not concentrate very much on it, and they are more likely to know things that very directly concern them than other more general matters. The example I always use is that farmers normally know a good deal about the farm program. The country would be better off if they did not.

As a general principle, voters are apt to be very asymmetrically informed, knowing a good deal about things where they are members of pressure groups, and not much about others. As an example of this, after Saddam had invaded the Kurd area and killed several thousand of his enemies, Clinton responded by dropping some bombs in the empty desert South of Baghdad. He also moved the no fly zone slightly to the North, but since the Iraqi air force is very poor this did not make much difference.

The probability is that this operation was much more damaging to the United States, in the sense that the bombs dropped were far more expensive than the damage inflicted by putting a few craters in the desert. Clinton regarded it as a striking counter blow, and I notice that most of the newspapers did so too. It indicated to Saddam and various other people of his general ilk that it is reasonably safe to kill friends of the United States.

Members of Congress must worry that they will have a bad image in the minds of voters, and this bad image may be not because they have done anything that would seriously annoy them, but the voters do not know what they have done. As a result of this congressmen make efforts to get information to the voter, but it is difficult, and particularly so since formal advertisements tend to be heavily discounted by the voter. Thus a good deal of random voting is done.

This randomness to a considerable extent is counterbalanced by the fact that people simply vote for a party without having any detailed idea of its specific policies. They are merely setting aside the information problem. The decision as to how to vote for an individual is a complex one. The voter can hardly make a correct decision in terms of any small collection of issues. The number of things that the congressman or president has done in the past period, and the things he is promising to do in the future, is very large. The voter is unlikely to know about most of them, and hence is likely to cast his vote in terms of what you might call the attitude of the politician.

Since all politicians make every effort to appear to have the right general attitude, regardless of what they are actually doing, this is not exactly a high precision instrument. What I have said is that the voters direct control over the congressmen is apt to be rather erratic. He is not put in a position to control and know most of the things the person he is judging does. Nevertheless, congressmen worry a great deal about him and what kind of information he has.

There was a book by Mann titled _Unsafe at Any Margin_[9] about how much congressmen do worry about this.

This does not mean that the voters are not influential for the congressman. He is fully aware of the fact that he requires their vote to stay in office. In the American context, he cannot simply sell out as he can in some other countries. The congressman then does his best to please the voters, granted, of course, that he is like all other human beings and has some non-instrumental motives. He may have charitable motives, or for that matter, he may have fallen in love with some particular person in his constituency whose views are radically different from the majority.[10] Mainly, however, he is simply trying to please the voters.

Of course, he is fully aware of how badly informed the voters are and is aware of the fact that to a considerable extent he can fool them. Fooling normally takes the form not of following his own personal ends, but trying to obtain the support of certain voters by doing things which the other voters would disapprove of and keeping it a secret from the other voters.

Keeping it a secret is usually quite easy because normally the reason the other voters would object is that it is some kind of expenditure for which they will have to pay the taxes. Since the tax amount per voter is very low for most projects they are not motivated to become well informed.

As an example the congressman may push for, let us say, a new post office in his district even if the mail volume is not enough to support it and the cost must hence come out of taxes. He calculates that the people who notice the new post office will remember and that people will not notice the new taxes, or more normally, that they did not receive a tax reduction. Politicians have a well deserved reputation for deviousness and lack of complete candor. This reputation is deserved, although a great many politicians do their best to appear to be open and candid people.

Basically, however, their maneuvers are not in general an effort to cheat all of their constituents, but an effort to benefit at least some of them at the expense, first, of people not in their constituency, and second, of other people in their constituency. Still, it is clear that the voters do indeed control the politicians. The politicians live in constant fear that the voters will throw them out.

From the voters standpoint the problem is that this fear tends to pressure politicians to specialize their attention on narrow special interest issues and in respect to more general issues leave it to others.

There is the fact that the individual politician normally hopes to have the reputation of being a conservative, liberal, socialist, libertarian, or something of that sort. In order to retain this reputation, he certainly will talk that way and he may on occasion use his political influence to get something through. There are cases in which the politician talks one way and votes another.

All of this is not intended to be a denunciation of either the politicians or the voters. Granted how little the influence any voter's vote has on the ultimate outcome, spending a lot of time to become well informed is hardly worth the trouble. Most voters have made this calculation, although professors of political science disapprove. On the other hand, politicians who are seriously interested in doing what the voters want are not necessarily interested in doing what the voters would want if they were better informed.

As a result of this, the total control exercised by the voters over the Congress is rather general. The average voter has a pretty good although vague idea of what the general position of any given member of Congress is. He knows whether he is liberal or not, possibly whether he is in favor of specific projects that will affect the voter, but on most of the things that the congressman votes on he is ignorant.

Granted the number of things that Congress votes on it is likely the congressman himself is not informed in detail of many aspects of the bills he votes on. The discussion of the federal soup kitchen earlier makes this clear since many of those things that are added to the bill at the last minute are known only to the congressman who asks it, and the congressman who grants it.

As a result of all this the control, although genuine and in fact vital to the congressman, is not precise in any sense. Once again we can turn to the private market on the same general area. No one would deny that the design of cars is vitally effected by what the designers think that the car buyers want. Nevertheless, most buyers do not know much about the details. I doubt that there is a single reader of this book, for example, can explain exactly how the steering gear of his car works. That is something upon which his life depends every day.

To say that voter control over the congressman's activity is far from precise is not a strong criticism. I can also say that the customers control of the details of things he buys is not precise. To a considerable extent I assume that the department stores I normally patronize have selected good quality merchandise which will meet my needs. Sometimes I am wrong. The same would be true with respect to a congressman, except it is more difficult for me to determine whether the policies that he votes for are to my advantage, than it is for me to determine whether a new pair trousers I have purchased is suitable.

The problem is that the different things that different members of the legislature feel will help them in the next election are complicated, messy, and non-identical. For example, the Department of Interior is devoted heavily to producing water projects in one sort or another in the west. These drew very little interest from the people in the rest of the country. The Tulsa ship canal, and the duplication of the Mississippi by another canal, were of very little interest to the people in the west.

Log-rolling bargains with respect to these issues required a good deal of subjective judgment, the ability to guess the intensity of the preferences of other people, etc. This was discussed earlier, but here we should point out that this makes it particularly difficult for the voters to control their representatives. Their representatives have a good deal of freedom in this kind of bargaining, and it should be said that they mainly use this freedom for the purpose of trying to improve their electoral chances.

In general, the net effect of this chapter has been that the control which the voters have over their representatives is strong but rather vague. In a real sense it is total. The representative can only remain a representative if he succeeds in solving all of these problems to the extent that his voters actually vote for him rather than for his opponent. Thus, we can say that the 'people rule' in the same sense that we could say that Louis XVI ruled France.

Louis XVI was a rather stupid man, and occasionally fell asleep at cabinet meetings. Nobody dared to wake him. Under the circumstances anything that he ordered would be done, but a good many things were done by other people in the absence of his orders. The voter control over our legislators is rather similar not because the voter is stupid, but unlike Louis XVI he cannot devote his entire working time to making political decisions.

The end product is not one of vigorous optimism. We can expect democracies will follow the 'will of the people', if we are willing to define 'will of the people' in a vague way. The people who object to this should suggest an alternative arrangement. If there has not been such an alternative arrangement suggested we must make do with what we have.

When there is a two-house legislature, as in the United States, the voter has the problem of getting exercising control through two channels. The members in the national legislature are elected by different ways in the two houses, and may respond to different constituencies. This makes voter control even less clear and direct.

There are sometimes cases in which the effort to have an agreement between the two houses leads to outcomes strongly contrary to the wishes of the people in each house, or at least, the wishes that they hope the voters will think they have. The standard rule in America is if there are differences between the two houses in a bill on the same subject, it is referred to a conference committee drawn from both houses. The result of this conference committee is a report which 'merges' the two proposals. It is put a vote and no amendments are permitted at that stage.

To repeat, there was a period of time in which people in both houses of Congress were attempting to get restrictions on Institute for Humanities prohibiting it from funding pornographic material. When put to vote in the form of an amendment in each house it always passed overwhelming with almost nobody voting against it. The bill, because of other differences in it, would then be sent to a conference committee, and the conference committee would remove this clause. This happened repeatedly, apparently because a good many members of the two legislatures wanted to appear publicly as being opposed to pornography, but actually didn't mind if it was 'high art'.

Earlier I discussed my log-rolling model which gives a clear-cut, straightforward, and symmetrical result, because it is clear-cut, straightforward and symmetrical in itself. The real world is messy. Still, there are a number of things that come out of the simple straightforward model, which are also characteristic of the more complicated world. Let us now turn to discussing the messy real world.

Normally log-rolling bargaining do not involve the identical item provided for each constituency like our road model. We mentioned before Congressman Udall's desire to put the Central Arizona Project through and his willingness to trade banning the development of Alaska, putting the farm subsidy program through, etc. Clearly, there is no simple straightforward way we can measure the exact value of each of these things either to Congressman Udall or the person with whom he is making trades. Under the circumstances the trading program will of necessity be messy.

Economists normally say that barter trade is much less efficient than money trade, and I shall not complain about that. Unfortunately, in most cases of political log-rolling we are forced to rely on barter trade because we are not permitted to make direct cash payments.[11] The inefficiency we would anticipate in barter trade occurs in the log-rolling bodies.

The inefficiency of barter trade does not mean there is none. Long ago, an Assyrian merchant community in Turkey maintained its records on baked clay tablets, and these tablets have survived. It is clear this was a prosperous merchant community, although there was no money. All transactions were by barter.

Once again these people were experts, and the people they dealt with were also experts. I think we can say that life would have been a good deal easier if they had single money, rather than depending on barter. The same is true in log-rolling.

This problem is so clear that mostly when we engage in theoretical investigations of log-rolling, we talk about direct cash payments. This is not because we think that it is a good idea, but because it makes the analysis much simpler.

If we turn to the real world it is messy and difficult, and there is no obvious reason to believe that the outcome is pareto optimal even though it is freely negotiated. This is true even if we ignore the people who are in the minority, i.e., who are outvoted. They are clearly injured, and there is a clear-cut externality.[12]

Here, as in so many other areas, we are confronted with a difficult problem for which the solution in actual use is inefficient. To say that it is inefficient is not to say that we know of a way of doing better. In this case we do not, although it would be nice if one of my readers would find one.

---

[1] Some of the dominions have weak upper houses also, apparently in an effort to copy England.

[2] New Zealand, Russia, and Italy have recently adopted a bizarre hybrid of the two systems copied from Germany.

[3] The 1880 census showed that Alabama had increased its share of the population, nevertheless, it lost a seat in Congress.

[4] They also have a president, but he is mainly a ceremonial figure.

[5] May 16, 1996, p.1.

[6] Prime Minister Wilson referred to this as a diminished mandate.

[7] They are almost all democrats.

[8] 1996 Was Year of Discontented Voter, Poll shows, by James Bennet, *The New York Times*, National, Friday, November 15, 1996.

[9] Mann, Thomas. *Unsafe at Any Margin: Interpreting Congressional Elections.* Washington: American Institute for Public Policy Research, 1978.

[10] This would be similar to John Stewart Mill and Harriet.

[11] There are some cases in which direct cash payments may be made, i.e., constituents of one congressman may for some special reason actually receive cash. This is most exceptional.

[12] See my 'Externalities and Government,' forthcoming in *Public Choice*.

CHAPTER 10
Voting, Different Methods and General Considerations

In earlier chapters I have argued that the American constitution is not particularly majoritarian. Let me now discuss the general issue of majoritarian votes. The first thing to be said is that if there are more than two possible alternatives, and there almost always are, then we have to discuss the method that actually guarantees a majority vote for one of them. For example, all alternatives will be submitted to the voters who each select one. The top two then go into a run off election. There are various other methods. These will be temporarily deferred. I will for the time being discuss the situation in which there are only two alternatives.

I have mentioned several cases in which I believe a minority would have lost in a simple majority vote, but it would be costly for them, and the gain for the winners would not be great. The Germans in 1933 would probably have voted for various discriminations against the Jews. In this particular area and almost throughout the entire reign of Stalin, there was mild discrimination against the Jews in Russia without any signs of public protest. At the very end Stalin had started his campaign to literally wipe them out. If he had lived another year the Jewish population would have been markedly smaller.[1]

Once again, there does not seem to be any signs of a popular opposition. Still, the ordinary Russian's willingness to discriminate against the Jews is not as plain as in the case of Germans, because after all there was no freedom of expression, while in Germany there had been before 1933.[2]

In order to avoid invidious comparisons, I should say that I was alive in the United States before World War II, and mild but genuine discrimination against Jews occurred quite regularly. Harvard, and the other leading schools had quotas for the number of Jews that they would admit, rather like today they have for Chinese and other orientals. There was nothing equivalent to affirmative action so within their quota they always selected the best candidates which may be one reason for the academic dominance of Jews today.[3]

All of this is vastly different from what we saw in Germany or Russia, but once again there was no sign of the population as a whole objecting to it, and it might well, if it come up, been voted into law by a majority. There are other cases. I mention again slavery in the early history of the United States, and indeed slavery throughout history. Up to about 1750 few thought slavery raised moral problems,[4] and opposition for moral reasons was generally regarded as eccentric.

For a modern example consider the position of prohibition in the United States. This went through in a constitutional manner, which means effectively much more than a simple majority, and it was eventually given up because it was realized there was a large number of people whose feeling against prohibition was strong enough so that they were willing to break the law. The people who favored prohibition apparently did not feel so strongly.

In all of these cases I believe there was a minority that felt strongly, and a majority which felt not so strongly. Thus a simple majority vote would inflict more injury through imposing difficulties for the minority than the gain to the majority. If we used the demand revealing process which permits people to express the intensity of their feelings as well as the direction, we can feel confident the outcome would have been the reverse.

Considering slavery, we can digress to wonder why the slaves were not simply bought by the abolitionists. It would have required some kind of credit operation to make this work out. In Greek and Roman times the law on slavery fluctuated a good deal, but during periods in which they were not at war, and hence there was not a free source of new slaves, it tended to be simple for a slave to purchase his own freedom. In essence, his master permitted him to buy it on credit, and the law was designed to make this easy. An old friend of mine, John Moes, put it that his body was more valuable to him than it was to anyone else because he had a sentimental attachment to it. He would be willing to work harder to pay off the mortgage on himself than as a slave.

Apparently something like this developed in the United States, because most of the southern states passed laws prohibiting freeing of slaves. In spite of these laws a number of profit-maximizing entrepreneurs like the owners of the Tredagar Iron Works in Richmond found it paid to violate the law, and give some of their employees their freedom in return for harder work. Needless to say the arrangement would not be legally enforceable, but the slave if he had raised the issue would have been held by the court simply to be a slave, because it was illegal in Virginia to free slaves.

It seems likely that one of the important reasons for the American south prohibiting freeing of slaves was the difference in skin color. In a society where almost all blacks were slaves it was difficult for a slave to simply move some place else, and act as a free citizen. Thus, prohibiting the development of a large free black community improved the protection of the property in the 'peculiar institution'. Here again we have a case which seems likely that simple majority voting would have given a result which inflicted more pain than the reverse result.

Of course you have the question of who should be permitted to vote which I have discussed before. As a quick review, until recently there were adults, sane, and with no criminal record, living in most democracies but unable to vote.[5] People may talk about requiring all adults to be able to vote as a necessary condition for democracy. Mostly they are perfectly willing to concede that Lincoln, who did not even have a majority, was a democratic President, and would be surprised if you told them that the United States, by their definition of democracy was not a democracy until the 1960s.

I will interject here that a rather sophisticated admirer of democracy said that it was a democracy if something approaching a majority of the adult population could vote. Women, in general, were not permitted to vote until World War I,[6] There were normally other small categories of people who could not vote, farm laborers in England, for example. Thus under his rule definition there would have been practically no genuine democracies until this century. Still, this definition clearly brings in Japan in 1941, and Germany in 1914. The view which is being pushed by many political scientists that democracies do not get into wars with other democracies, with this definition is clearly untrue.

Let us think about these matters a little and assume that the demand revealing process or some other procedure is imposed so that people can weigh their preferences. It is possible that an arrangement to purchase the Southern slaves and free them subject to a fairly large special tax to reimburse the Federal government for payment to their masters would have achieved general approval in the United States any time after 1820. Of course the Northern abolitionists were violently opposed to paying anything for the slaves, although obviously purchasing them all and freeing them without any compensation whatsoever would have been much cheaper than the Civil War.

This has been a digression. Let us go to the problem of obtaining a simple majority when there are more than two possible alternatives. If we are to guarantee a majority there must be some procedure to reduce the number of alternatives to two, and this procedure may have a number of fairly severe difficulties.

Let me begin with something suggested by Lewis Carroll which was simply that if there was no majority the voting be suspended for a short period of time while the people thought the matter over and discussed it. Then another vote held. It was apparently intended that his process would be continued until a majority was obtained or everybody gave up.

It could be said that where there is no majority we just will not enact anything, but this sneaks another alternative in. Doing nothing in the area is always a possibility, and logically should be put into the voting series as it is in terms of the final vote in all parliamentary procedures. Doing nothing if there is no single majority vote is equivalent to agreeing with one of the alternatives and giving that alternative, doing nothing, a superior position. We will see shortly that something like this is quite common.

I pause here and summarize what I take it is the current conventional wisdom among students in the area. Since I myself agree with it, the term 'conventional wisdom' in this case is not intended to be an insult.

There is no known voting method which can be said to guarantee a majority which is not the result of random factors, like order of voting if there are many alternatives, and the preferences are reasonably diverse. We can arrange things in such a way that the alternatives are winnowed down, and there is eventually only a pair. Then there can be a choice by majority vote. The winnowing down process, and we will turn to that in a moment, is subject to so many difficulties that referring to the winner as having a majority over all of the other alternatives, is simply foolish.

One of the standard methods of cutting down the alternatives to two, which is familiar to most Americans, is to have two major parties and have each of them put up their candidates or policies. The founding fathers were strongly opposed to parties, but we have during most of our history two fairly strong parties. They change from time to time. The Republicans did not exist before 1854. There normally have been a number of minor parties, like prohibitionist, socialist, etc.

Up until the 1968 election it was legally extremely difficult for anyone except for the two main parties to get on the ballot. Wallace as part of his presidential campaign conducted an intensive and intelligent set of legal actions with the result that this blockade which in essence had been enacted by the two parties as a sort of cartel restriction has been lifted. Since then third parties have been not very successful, but at least possible. Wallace, himself, John Anderson, and Perot have succeeded in getting on the ballot throughout the country and getting a significant number of votes. Further, a number of minor parties like the Libertarians have taken advantage of this to get on the ballot throughout most of the country even though they do not get a great number of votes.

The presidential candidates are largely elected by a very confused primary process running from state to state with people in the later-voting states tending to be really left out of the process. Primaries have only recently become dominant in Presidential choice, but have been for a long time common at a lower level. In this case the members of two separate parties vote among themselves for whom will represent them in the upcoming election. If we confine ourselves to these parties alone, this does not guarantee us a sensible contest. Goldwater and McGovern both obtained nominations in their own parties although in both cases they were obviously doomed before the campaign even began.[7]

I have not here gone through every single method that is used to whittle the choice down to two so that we are guaranteed a majority, however I do not think that anyone will question my view that all of them have fairly severe defects from a strict majoritarian perspective.[8] Of course, as mentioned in the first chapter, Americans tend to take anything we are accustomed to as being equivalent to majority voting.

There is by the way another procedure that is used in a few countries to obtain a majority in the legislature even if not elsewhere. In these countries whichever party gets the largest number of members of the legislature (say the Democrats had 40 percent, the Republicans 35, and Perot's followers 25 percent of the members of the House) would be given a bonus set of seats in order to guarantee it a majority. This, of course, is totally different from our procedures and it is hard to argue that it is the result truthfully of an election process, but it does guarantee a majority in the legislature as long as party discipline holds up.

I now turn to a very common method which for some obscure reason I do not think that most people realize is a solution to the above problem, even if it is not a wonderfully good solution. I turn again to the referendum process. This is actually a choice between two alternatives; the proposed a referendum and doing nothing. Normally, either the act proposed gets a majority or in many cases something more than a simple majority, say two-thirds, or the status quo remains in effect. Thus, we have a choice between two alternatives and if the proposal or the status quo wins, this solves the problem.[9]

There are two technical problems. The first is that the order in which the voting is undertaken can be very important. The second is that there is no obvious reason why the one that is accepted could not, when it became a part of the status quo, be beaten by one of the ones that had not been presented to the voters. This is in a way a restatement of the first objection.

A variant on this is the basic method that democracy uses in dealing with policy questions, and as we shall see below it was used to some extent by Venice in dealing with elections. It is also the basic method that is used by the parties in selecting the presidential candidate, although in that case it is concealed.

It used to that be the actual decision was made in the presidential nominating conventions, and this sometime required a large number of votes. 124 in one democratic convention when they required a two-thirds majority to nominate.[10] Today it is simply a bit of history.

If we look at legislation we find that something like what I have just described occurs. A complex proposal usually has many, many different clauses, pork scattered around among the constituencies, etc., and when it is brought to Congress, it is either voted up, or voted down. If we consider only that one vote, there is no Arrow problem. But the actual bill presented must be chosen by some other process.[11]

Once again it would be possible to go through a vast collection of amendments, sub-amendments, etc., but that is not what happens. It is true that in the Senate there are sometimes a number of amendments offered, but basically the bill is produced by somebody, not necessarily the relevant committee, it may be the leadership or even the leadership in the minority party. As produced, it is already a complex matter, and there are not very many changes actually voted on. Basically, it is voted up or voted down.

There is a great deal of careful anecdotal historical research about particular bills by political scientists. They do not seem to have any theory except one offered by Shepsley which is that the committee makes up its mind and then if it makes the proper trades, it will go through. There are several problems with this, one of which is the committee itself is a voting body, and we simply move from one voting body to another. Shepsley, in private conversation, answered this by saying that the chairman actually controlled it. I do not believe that but it is true the chairman has more influence than the average member.

In fact, only a few of the possible alternatives will actually be put before the legislature, normally only one, and that one will either pass or fail, because that is the way voting is run. The process reduces the alternatives to two, refusing to consider many possibilities in the voting process.

I am not alleging that the committees systematically eliminate alternatives which are better than the ones that they finally end up with. What I am alleging is that no one (including committee members) knows how they reach their conclusion, and we do not know whether some of the alternatives that are eliminated in the discussion inside committee might not beat the one they finally adopt. There is possibly a different distribution of post offices which would get it through it at a lower cost. There are a collections of potential loopholes in the federal income tax law which might purchase more votes than the present ones. We simply do not know.

What we do know is the people who do this in the committees, and for that matter in the leadership and on the floor, are reasonably skilled, but they do not have complete information about the preferences of the other people who will be voting. Nor do we actually know how they make their decisions.

Is there weighted voting with weights vary from time to time? If one person who feels strongly, can he impose something on other people who object to it, but not very strongly? We do not know with respect to any given bill, although the careful empirical study by the political scientists might give us a pretty good idea with respect to those particular bills which have been studied. They are a very small minority of all bills.

Going further I would like to talk briefly about a suggestion of Dennis Mueller called 'voting by veto'. In this system all of the people are qualified to vote. Let us assume that the 435 members of the House of Representatives each propose a motion on some particular subject. There are now 435 motions, plus the status quo or 436 total alternatives. Each individual[12] then selects one of this mass of alternatives and vetoes it. After 435 vetoes there will be one left which could be the status quo, or one of the others.

Mueller's argument for this is not that it gets the ideal outcome. Granted this system, all of the 435 are motivated to try propose propositions which will not be vetoed by any single member of the remaining 434. He feels this would mean that all of the decisions would be 'moderate'.

Note, this is not necessarily a wonderful voting method, but it at least tells us where the various propositions come from. The individual congressmen would need very good ideas as to the prejudice of other people. In other words, their preference functions would not actually be independent of each other and the mathematics which assumes independence is invalid here. Further, it is not particularly likely that any of the proposed alternatives would actually be the first choice of anybody.

The reason that I have brought this up, is I believe what actually goes on in the legislative before it gets the floor does have some resemblance to this. I believe that general ideas are suggested, and then individual members of the house leadership, etc. switch their votes on receipt of various special favors. They could either vote for or against in return for payment.

It is not necessary to get everybody in, the majority will do, or in the Senate 60 percent, and it will be sensible to consider both Houses and the President. The whole process, including the conference committees should be taken into account by the people attempting to get some general program through.

This is a realistic account of what happens, and it will be seen that it is not very closely duplicated by the existing mathematical theory. Further, it is extremely difficult to test empirically because the individual congressman will be voting for the whole package of items, and each congressman may in fact be motivated by the fact that he likes one particular sub-part of the packet, and dislikes another. Another congressman who also likes one sub-packet and dislikes the another may have different packets.

So far the readers may think that I have led them into an impasse, and I do not quarrel with that judgment. The existing theory of voting, is more straightforward than this. My point has been that this simple straightforward theory we now have is only part of the entire theory which we should hope to have. The major aspiration of this book is to stimulate research in areas where at the moment we do not know very much. I regret that I have to admit I am merely suggesting research. I can not offer an idea of my own on how to engage in this research. Nevertheless, I think such research is highly desirable.

It will not surprise any student in this area, but I think that I should emphasize that matters of agenda control, the order of which things are voted on, are as important as the actual voting. I would like to give one striking example. When the United Nations was first organized, the interests of the Union of South Africa in the United Nations were taken care of by Great Britain. At substantially every meeting of the United Nations a proposal was made condemning South Africa. The British arranged that it was far enough down the agenda so that it was never voted on.

After a while a South African foreign minister who was more interested in his domestic political position than in the wellbeing of South Africa wanted to go to the UN and make a speech. He insisted that the South African matter be moved up to the top of the agenda, made his speech and harvested an almost unanimous resolution of condemnation. From that meeting on South Africa was condemned at each meeting of the UN General Assembly. This was a particularly striking example of intelligent agenda control by the British representatives, and hopelessly stupid agenda control by the Foreign Minister of South Africa. Of course it may have improved his political standing in South Africa, and that may have been his major objective.

There are now journals specializing in public choice. Mainly they run articles in what has been called normal science as opposed to revolutionary science. This is not a criticism as most sciences are in the normal step-by-step process, and we owe the great advances we now have over Egypt 3,000 B.C. to this step-by-step process. Still, we would like radical improvements.

I am not in a position to recommend any particular radical improvement, although I would like them. For the time being all that I can predict is continuing our step-by-step progress. We undeniably have made considerable progress by this method. I would like to close by pointing out that we have already made a good start, everyone should hope for radical improvements. Everyone should keep their eyes open in the hope that they will find them.

---

[1] His campaign highlighted Jewish doctors. It is conceivable that the campaign accelerated his death by removing Jews from his personal medical staff.

[2] Hitler did not actually win the election before he came into power, but he did well, and his original rise to power was completely constitutional. Needless to say, he did not find the constitution a serious hindrance once he got power.

[3] The orientals probably will have the same dominance in the next generation.

[4] Both Alexander Hamilton and Benjamin Franklin were members of abolition societies. The dropped their scruples at the constitutional convention. Jefferson and Madison were both slaveowners, in Jefferson's case, on a large scale.

[5] You may not like using the term democracy for the United States in let say 1789, but once again this book is about voting, not about meaning of democracy.

[6] They did not receive full franchise in England until the 1931 election.

[7] In the case of McGovern this may not be true. He campaigned as a far left Democrat having made remarks to reporters and so forth that it was harder to get nominated in a Democratic Party than it was to win the election. As soon as he was nominated he made an effort to shift sharply to the right, but discovered that because of the things he had said in his nominating campaign he could not pull it off. Thus he probably thought

that the position of the far left he assumed in order to get the Democratic nomination would not handicap him later in the Presidential election itself, although of course it did.

[8] This is true no matter how many votes are needed for election.

[9] In Arizona, judges are periodically subjected to an election process in which the voters vote for their continuance in office or their removal. This is rather like the referendum voting process.

[10] This was to protect the democratic solid south from unfriendly president.

[11] I have been reading *The New York Times*, as I write this book, and the front page carried a box about the bizarre things that had gotten into the main spending bill of the session. On Page 12 there was another collection on the same topic as a continuation of the box. One of the items contained in this appropriation bill was intended to settle a quarrel between Rhode Island and the Narraagansett Indian tribe. People responsible for all of this boasted that they had only accepted half of the proposals made by individual members of Congress. There does not seem to have been any formal voting process any where in this selection. October 3, 1996.

[12] The order of which they are called might be important, but we will ignore the matter here.

APPENDIX
A Bouquet of Voting Methods

I will here discuss a list of different voting methods that have been used in various places. It will not be a complete listing. To be complete would take much more space than this book, but it will give you an idea of the variety of the voting methods which are possible.

Let me begin with the voting method which Aristotle thought was the most stupid he had heard of. In this procedure the judges of the election were moved into a room which was next to an open square where the voting took place, but the window overlooking into the square was high enough so that the judges could not see the voters. The voters then assembled in the square, and various candidates were brought in and the voters cheered. The judges would decide which candidate had the loudest cheers, and that would be the one elected.

To repeat, Aristotle thought this was the most stupid method, but we Americans would tend to think that the method which was very common all over the Mediterranean at the time was equally bad; voting by tribes. The citizens of Rome, let us say, in their assembly would line up by their tribes, and each tribe would cast a vote according to the desires of a majority of the people then present from the tribe. The actual outcome would then depend on the majority of the tribes. This would permit three people who were the only representatives of one tribe to cast as powerful a vote as say 200 representing another. It resembled the American senate in this respect.

Let us turn from this election system to the one which substantially any historical investigation would show up as the best. Venice had only a very slowly changing constitution from about 800 to Napoleon's conquest of it around 1800 A.D., roughly 1,000 years. It was stable, had no coups, and gave what was generally thought to be the best government in Europe at the time. Of course the competition was not exactly stiff.

Further, a city which consisted essentially of a sand bar not only became a great and wealthy trading nation but built up a sizeable empire, and was able to take on great powers in war. Altogether, it was a very successful government and to this day the city in the lagoons is one of the most beautiful places in the world in spite of its very unfavorable situation. Its art and architecture more than make up.

The highest official in the Venetian government was the Doge, and his election after about 1200 A.D. followed a procedure which we are likely today to find rather odd.

> The ducal election lasted five days, with two stages of the process allotted to each day. Thirty members of the Great Council, exclusive of patricians under thirty years of age, were selected by lot. Retiring to a separate chamber, this group of thirty reduced themselves by lot to nine, who then elected forty men by a majority of at least seven votes each. After electing the forty, the nine returned to the hall of the Great Council with their list of nominees, 'without looking at, speaking or making a sign to anyone'. (Sanuto, *Cronachetta*, p.71.)

> These nominees were announced to the chamber and checked to insure that no clan had more than one representative, a precaution followed at every stage of the election. The group of forty assembled in a separate room and reduced their number by sortition to the twelve men who were to elect the next group of twenty-five by at least seven votes apiece; although forbidden to nominate themselves, the twelve could elect a member of the previous

group of forty. The twenty-five were reduced by lot to nine, who elected forty-five patricians by the usual majority of seven votes. The forty-five drew lots to select eleven of their number, and the Eleven (the *Undici*) elected the Forty-one (the *Quarantuno*) that then elected the doge by at least twenty-five votes.'[1]

The actual election was not carried on as we would expect. The 41 each wrote down a name and put it in a jar. One was drawn. The person that was drawn, if he was a member of the group, and any of his relatives if they were members of the 41 left, and the remainder discussed his qualifications. After a suitable period of time he was brought back in, and would answer questions, and perhaps make a short speech. If he then received 25 votes he was the Doge, if he did not another name was drawn. You will note that the majority is roughly 60 percent. In general, somebody within the original 41 names would be elected Doge, but if no one was then the process would be repeated.

It is not only there that above majority voting was used in Venice. The rules were complicated 'motions to alter electoral procedures or grant petitions often required a favorable vote of two-thirds, three-fourths, or even five-sixths of the patricians present in the assembly'.[2] The reader will no doubt noticed that none of these methods involved placing one proposal against another. They involved taking up proposals one at a time, and putting them against the status quo. The status quo in the case of the election is that there was no Doge.

The use of random allocation in the election of the Doge had the basic purpose of preventing the type of factualism which tore most Italian cities apart. It was successful for many centuries.

These were unusual forms of voting, although certainly the success of the organizations which used them is a strong argument in their favor. Even today we do not feel as confident in the strength of our armed forces as did the citizens of the Roman Republic.

Now, let us turn to other kinds of voting. The first one I would like to discuss is one in which the different voters have different numbers of votes. The obvious case of this is the British House of Commons before 1830. This came from essentially a minor accident in the way the thing was designed.

The seats in Parliament were held by various districts and constituencies, each of which had two. In general, these constituencies had been designed a long time before, and their populations were not equal. The House of Pitt actually owned six seats in the House of Commons by owning the real estate upon which the alleged cities or districts existed. They among other things owned the famous Old Sarum which was a plowed field that sent two members to Parliament. Other members of the aristocracy also held many votes, but there were actually a few places where a sizeable number of people voted for their representative.

Burke in the earlier part of his career represented Bristol which had over 4,000 voters, and was the most populous constituency. He voted against certain changes in the tax law which would greatly benefit Bristol. His citizens threw him out, and he spent the rest of his career representing a rotten borough.

Anyone seeking amusement as well as information is advised to read Namier's *Structure of British Politics at the Accession of George III*.[3] It is essentially a listing of the various constituencies in England with all that Namier could find about how they sent their representatives to Parliament. The one that impressed me most was one in which public spirited citizens in northern constituency put their two seats of Parliament up to auction. The money derived was used to repair roads in the constituency. Other tales in Namier's book are perhaps not quite so amusing, but they do indicate that popular voting was not exactly the norm.

I have already mentioned that the power of the voters varies a good deal in the American Senate. Probably the place in which inequality of voters is most common is in the election of the board of directors of a corporation. It is of some interest that this system actually comes from about the same time that Burke was having difficulty with the voters of Bristol.

Lord Clive, being a wealthy man, bought a lot of stock in the Honorable East India Company and talked some of his friends into doing so too. They divided their stock up among a number of their friends who could be depended upon to vote as they wished and return the stock after a while. At this time all stock holders simply had one vote. Clive and his friends were called 'splitters.' Opponents also split, but as a result corporations began providing that there was one vote per share instead of one vote per head. In any event, today almost all corporations are arranged in such a way that you get as many votes as you have shares.

The existence of 'corporate democracy' is frequently doubted because it is certainly true that the stockholders[4] pay little attention to their corporation's business. If they become unhappy with it normally they just sell their stock rather than waiting until the next election and voting against the current board. Still, stockholder approval, which is mainly in terms of profits, is absolutely vital to the management.

The reason that it is vital to the management is not that usually there will be stockholder efforts to throw the management out, but that the existence of stockholder dissatisfaction whether it is indicated by selling the stock, which means that the stock declines in value, or by just complaining, means that there is an opportunity for a corporate raider.

The raiders will, if they decide that some corporation is not producing adequate profit, try and buy it out, fire the present management, put a new management in. Then when the stock goes up, they sell it and go on to another corporation. This is a mechanism first explicated by Henry Manne is the basic way that corporations work.

In the United States for a long time this was very easy, in other countries, Germany and Japan for example, this was hard to do with the result that their corporations were not as continuously pressed to behave in a profit maximizing manner as ours were.

The managements of corporations, needless to say, do not like this system and they have over the years developed various methods of trying to make it hard to buy the corporation's stock and fire them. Ignoring temporarily those things that are done by the corporation itself, one of the things that they have done is attempt to get various governments to pass rules making it difficult.

Interestingly enough, in recent years they have succeeded in sneaking some provisions providing for super tax into the federal government corporation and individual income tax. These special provisions raise substantially no money, but they do mean that it is harder to throw an inefficient corporate management out, and hence reduce the total efficiency of our economy to some extent.

Mainly countries use voting systems in which the people who can vote have only one vote apiece. Not everybody can vote, for example the House of Lords in England. The equivalents that have been appointed in Australia and Canada are not elected officials, nor, for that matter, are the members of the Supreme Court of the United States, who are probably more important in our government than the House of Representatives.

We now turn to more normal methods of voting, at least more normal in the present day. The first of these is what I call the English system in which the legislature is selected by voting in each constituency. Normally one person will be selected to represent that constituency, whether that constituency is the state of California, the state of Alaska in the senate, or a more or less equal sized constituency in the House. We already discussed at some length the way that this kind of thing can go wrong because of the fact that there may be more than two candidates. On the other hand, the whittling down to two can go badly wrong. This has been adequately discussed before, but the reader should keep it in mind.

Another method which has gained some approval is approval voting. The voter is confronted with a list of possible nominees, and marks those that are above his minimum requirement, i.e., those that he approves. This has been discussed together with the strategic methods of cheating on it earlier on in the book, and there is not much to add here, except that it is very convenient for the learned societies that face some kind of rebellion.

The rebels might conceivably get more first choice votes than the members of the establishment who are nominated by the society, but most people will approve of the members of the society who are nominated, and not all of them will approve of the rebels. In consequence, the establishment will normally win. I believe this is the reason that it has been adopted by a number of the learned societies.

The second method that I would like to discuss is proportional representation, but before I begin discussing it as it exists in general in the world, I would like to talk about two systems which no longer exist, and one purely theoretical proposal that I have made and another made by Tollison etc.

First is one that was used in Illinois when I was a boy. The lower house of the legislature was elected three to a constituency. The voters had three votes which could be cast either one vote for each of three people, one and a half for each of two people, or three votes for one person. Illinois was mainly on the two party system and the two parties did have pretty much control over who ran for their seats in the legislature.

The system provided a strategic problem. Rockford, where I was brought up, was primarily, but not entirely a Republican city and for a long time the Republican Party nominated two, both of whom were elected and the Democrats also two, but only one of them would be elected. At one point the Republicans became ambitious and nominated three and the Democrats stuck to two with the result that the two Democrats were elected and only one of the three Republicans, although to repeat the Republicans outnumbered

Democrats at that time and place. As far as I know this system has never been used anywhere else although something like it has recently been adopted by some cities in the south.[5] The second system that I would like to talk about was developed in Japan and I have no idea exactly how it got started. It was a function of the post-war Japanese constitution, not the pre-war. In this case they had constituencies most of which would send more than one representative to the legislature, three to five on average. Voters all had one vote and the consequence of this was that the representatives of the various parties in essence competed with each other because the party discipline was not by any means perfect.

It resulted in the development of the cliques, which so dominated Japanese politics. The Liberal Democrats, for example, were actually a sort of federation of cliques. The clique leader raised money for campaigning and his followers campaigned in some, usually not all of the constituencies, against the followers of other leaders. It seems to me that in silliness it competes with the Greek system mentioned above. It has now been replaced by a different system that we will discuss below and until at least one or two elections have been run under the new system the outcome is quite unpredictable.

We now return to the types of proportional representation I mentioned above. The first one which I invented and put in *Toward a Mathematics of Politics*[6] is simply that the members of the legislature have different numbers of votes depending on how many people have voted for them. I went further and assumed that we have computers and people could quickly change their representative at any time. The present system developed in the late middle ages in which many high political figures actually could not do simple arithmetic.[7] It does not seem to have much argument for it except that it is easy if you do not have computers. With computers there is no reason why each member of the legislature should have the same number of votes or why people cannot change their representative from time to time.

To go farther as I did earlier it is quite possible to have many more representatives than can sit in one room. In the article I actually suggested that since my mother was retired and living in Florida, that my sister and I and her husband could all designate my mother as our representative and she could sit and watch the proceedings on television and from time to time cast four votes.

Whether or not you think that this is a good idea, it is certainly feasible today. I would argue that the proportional representation systems that I will discuss below are in essence rather crude efforts to reach something like that system.

The next system that I would like to turn to was invented by Robert Tollison.[8] In this case by an ingenious and radical technique each person was guaranteed an equal weight in government in the sense that they would actually be able to put at least some bills through. For example a clique of ten percent of the voters, if they lost on one issue would have the weight of their votes automatically increased for the next vote and so on, until eventually this ten percent got their will even if their position was different from everyone else. In other words the number of bills passed by each individual clique would be roughly its own strength, although they could get together either formally or informally.

Neither of the two above systems have been used, but proportional representation is in fact in use in general throughout the world and I would like to begin with the version that was discussed by Lewis Carroll. Originally that was what was meant by proportional representation, but now it is only used in a few odd places like Cambridge, Massachusetts, Australia, and Ireland. It was also adopted in New York for the regional school boards and has caused a great deal of trouble.

In this system you have, let us say, five openings on a board to be elected. Various people run and the voter is required to rank all the people that run from first preference, second preference, etc. on down. The method in which the votes are counted is rather complicated and in early days meant that the votes took almost an infinite amount of time to be computed. Now with computers it is fairly fast, but New York when it adopted the system for the school boards apparently did not know that computers existed and hence the long delays in finding out who won is one of the complaints about it.

Basically, if there are five people to be elected, and ten candidates, the first choices of all the voters are looked at and if any one of the candidates has one-sixth plus one of the votes that person is declared elected. The one sixth plus one is called the droop quota. Normally this candidate would have more than just one-sixth plus one and hence some of his votes would be switched to his second choice.

The exact way in which this is done varies. Let us assume that it is done randomly. The counting is then is done again and if there is somebody else with the 'droop quota' mentioned above he is declared elected and the same process goes through.

Normally eventually we will reach a situation in which there are no excess votes to be distributed. At that point the candidate with the least votes is eliminated and his votes are distributed to his second preference. All of this is continued until five people have been elected. For some reason this system seems to be quite popular, but I have never understood why. It means not that everybody has a choice particularly, but that everybody's vote somewhere or other will be counted. It may however be counted to give somebody that he detests, but is not from his standpoint the worst person on the ballot. On the other hand it is quite possible that somebody's vote would be involved in electing his first, second and third choices. To call this equal seems to me bizarre.

To repeat, this is in fact used in a few places and in general, in places where they come fairly close to having a two party system, with the result that the system does not have all that bad an effect. The New York school board situation is in this respect exceptional.

Another form of proportional representation is very widely used and it has already been described briefly in the earlier part of the book. One or another variant of it, and we will discuss three here, is used in a clear majority of democracies. In all three a number of different legislative seats are grouped together in one large bundle. In some cases the number is the entire membership of the lower house of the legislature, and in other cases it is perhaps 15 to 20 legislators. The parties then nominate candidates for these positions, and the nomination procedure is usually informal and need not be discussed here. The voter then checks one party.

The parties then receive the same share of the total number of seats in the legislature to their share of the vote. Thus the legislature will have the same percentage of people from each party as in the population.[9] This system provides what is sometimes referred to as a 'mirror of the people'. More often than not it produces more than two parties in the legislature, although not always.

If no party gets a majority which is a common event, some kind of compromise coalition has to be hammered together. It is rather like the situation of the United States when the President is of one party, and the two houses of legislature the other. In that event there is no true party control.

In most cases the members of the legislature are appointed by simply going to the top of the list of names that the party has submitted, and going down the appropriate number. If there are 20 seats in this particular district, and the given party has received one-quarter of the votes, it will get 5 seats, and these will be the 5 at the top of the list. This gives the party machine a great deal of power, and in most cases it is exercised rather arbitrarily. There does not seem to be any case in which the government has insisted that this be dealt with by a primary, or something of that sort.

There are two places in which the voters have more say than what I have described above. In Switzerland, you can go down the list of your favorite party, and strike out 1 or maybe 2 of the names. You then write above the names you struck out, the name of another candidate on the list who you particularly favor. The candidates who are actually selected will be determined by those voters who have taken the trouble to do this rather than by the party machine.

If the party had 25 percent of the votes, and was going to get 5 out of 20 representatives, those 5 would be the ones that had the most of these 'cumulation' votes by individuals.

This system is interesting as it turns out not very many of the voters bother to cumulate. This means that those voters who are particularly interested in politics are much more powerful than those who are not. It is a self-selection in terms of political interest and probably the voters who cumulate are better informed than the others. In a way we have a voluntary division of the voters into two categories, an upper and a lower, with anybody who wishes to spend a little extra time voting, being in the upper.

Italy had, until the recent reforms, a system in which you were permitted in addition to marking the party on the ballot to simply check five of its nominees, and the number of such checks was used to select who would actually occupy that party's seats. This system had a peculiar by-product. The Communist Party was highly disciplined during most of its history, although not now, and designated who individual voters would vote for. By telling the voters a separate combination of which ones they were to check they were able to tell whether each had in fact carried out instructions. You could simply inspect the ballot and see whether the combination assigned to a given party member had occurred.

Germany after World War II, when they drew up their new constitution, produced a compromise between the single member constituency and the proportional representation, which I think has nothing to say for it, but it has been copied by Italy, New Zealand, Japan, and Russia.

Under this system something like half of the members of the legislature are elected in the constituencies according to the English system described above. The other half are elected by proportional representation. Each citizen casts two votes, one for the candidate from his constituency and the other a proportional vote for the party. The result of these are two quite disparate bodies of candidates who have been elected, but they meet in the same hall and vote in the ordinary way. To repeat what I have said above I cannot think of anything much to be said for this except that it is a compromise. This in my opinion bizarre procedure has been copied by New Zealand, Japan, and Russia. Apparently they all like compromised and do not know very much about voting theory.

Personally, I would like a two chamber legislature with one chamber elected according to the English system and the other according to the proportional representation system. The reader can immediately say that I too am a compromiser, and in a way I am. The compromise is not between these two forms of voting, however. I would like a more than majority, two-thirds to three-quarters to pass bills. It seems very difficult to talk people into even considering this, but I think that my two house legislature raised in this way might be more readily saleable politically. It would have the same net effect because the two-house members being elected differently would require effectively more than 50 percent of the population to elect a majority in both houses. Thus I am compromising, but a different compromise than the one that I criticized above.

I obviously should not leave this topic without mentioning my favorite form of voting, which is demand revealing. This is a system which permits the individual to indicate the intensity of his desires. Since the Nobel Prize has just been awarded to a man who did some preliminary work in this area, I suppose it is more popular than it used to be, but basically no one has actually adopted it except for a few American bureaucracies where the actual inventor, Ed Clark, was employed. I am not going to go through it here because I have written so much on it before.[10] Basically, his system means that you indicate how strongly you feel, as well as what alternative you favor. It is a very clever system which makes it unwise for you to misinform people as to the intensity of your preferences. To repeat, I am not going to discuss this here. There is plenty of material in print on it, and it does not seem likely that it will be widely adopted in the near future.

There are a number of other voting methods which have been suggested, Mueller's voting by veto for example, an exhaustive list would take another book, so I will stop here. If the reader is still curious, I should warn him that research in the field is both tedious and likely to be erroneous. Basic sources frequently misdescribe voting methods for reasons that are mysterious to me. In any event, I leave it here.

---

[1] *Politics in Renaissance Venice*, by Robert Finlay, Rutgers University Press, New Brunswick, New Jersey, p.140.

[2] *Politics in Renaissance Venice*, by Robert Finlay, Rutgers University Press, Rutgers, 1980, p.141.

[3] Namier, Lewis Bernstein, Sr. *The Structure of Politics at the Accession of George III.* New York: St. Martin's and London: Macmillan (1957).

[4] Including me.

[5] See 'All for One' by Samuel Issacharoff and Richard H. Pildes, *The New Republic*, Nov. 18, 199, p.10.

[6] Tullock, Gordon. *Toward a Mathematics of Politics.* Chapter 10. Ann Arbor: University of Michigan Press (1967).

[7] Hence the court of the exchequer.

[8] Mueller, Dennis, Tom Willit, and Robert Tollison. 'On Equalizing the Distribution of Political Influence' *Journal of Political Economy* (March/April 1974): 414–22.

[9] There are problems of rounding error here, and there are various ways of dealing with them. None of them are very successful, but none of them are disastrous.

[10] Nicholas Tideman and Tullock 'A New and Superior Method of Election.' *Journal of Political Economy* 84(6) (October 1976): 1145-59. The reader can easily find out how it works there.

INDEX